CAMBRIDGE CL

General Editors

F. M. CORNFORD, D. S. ROBERTSON, F. E. ADCOCK

I
ZENO OF ELEA

CAMBRIDGE
UNIVERSITY PRESS

University Printing House, Cambridge CB2 8BS, United Kingdom

Cambridge University Press is part of the University of Cambridge.

It furthers the University's mission by disseminating knowledge in the pursuit of
education, learning and research at the highest international levels of excellence.

www.cambridge.org
Information on this title: www.cambridge.org/9781107480278

© Cambridge University Press 1936

First published 1936
First paperback edition 2014

A catalogue record for this publication is available from the British Library

ISBN 978-1-107-48027-8 Paperback

ZENO OF ELEA

A Text, with Translation and Notes

BY

H. D. P. LEE

Fellow and Tutor of Corpus Christi
College, Cambridge

CAMBRIDGE

AT THE UNIVERSITY PRESS

1936

My thanks are due to Professor Cornford for the help he has given me at every stage of this work.

H. D. P. L.

CONTENTS

INTRODUCTION

The object of this study is not so much to expound the philosophy of Zeno as, by means of a collection of the relevant information, to present as a whole what there is to be expounded. Zeno is most widely known as the author of the four famous arguments on motion; and anyone who has read any part of what has been written about him cannot fail to notice that by far the greater part of it is concerned with these four arguments. They are no doubt the most intriguing and the most important part of his philosophy; but none the less too great a concentration on them cannot fail to give a one-sided view. And, though in histories[1] of Greek thought less one-sided accounts are to be found, yet it seemed worth while to put together a text containing the relevant information and so get a view of what we know of Zeno's philosophy as a whole. For, though it is now realised that Zeno is a figure of first importance not only in the history of Greek philosophy, but in the history of philosophy in general, the collections of the texts giving his arguments that have been made up to the present time[2] are far from exhaustive.

With the exposition or solution of the logico-mathematical difficulties involved in Zeno's arguments I am not concerned; I have not, in any case, the requisite knowledge or skill. I have merely attempted to give as complete a text of Zeno as possible, and to explain in a brief commentary what exactly the arguments were as Zeno expounded them. If it is objected that my knowledge of mathematics is inadequate, I can only reply that Zeno

---

[1] As e.g. in Burnet, *E.G.P.*[3]; Tannery, *Science Hellène*; Milhaud, *Philosophes-Géomètres*; Zeller, *Pre-Socratic Philosophy*.

[2] Diels, *Vorsokratiker*, of course gives the most complete.

was as ignorant of modern mathematics as I am; and I think it arguable that one whose mind is not prejudiced by modern mathematical ideas is the more likely to attain historical accuracy.[1]

AUTHORITIES

We may divide the information about Zeno of Elea which has come down to us into two kinds. There are, firstly, paraphrases or actual quotations of his arguments, or what are alleged to be his arguments: and there is, secondly, information about his life and his writings and their general nature and purpose. The object of my collection of passages is to give a conspectus of the relevant information of the first kind. For the second kind I shall assume that the collection

[1] Bibliographical note. A great deal of the literature about Zeno which I have consulted is devoted to the solution of the logical difficulties raised by his arguments, and I am therefore not concerned with it. From a more historical point of view the following are relevant:

Brochard, V., *Études de Philosophie Ancienne et Moderne* (first two articles = *Séances et Travaux de l'Acad. des Sc. Mor. et Pol.* N.S. XXIX. 1888, I. pp. 555–68; *Rev. Mét. et Mor.* I. 1893, pp. 209–15).
Burnet, *Early Greek Philosophy* (ed. 3), pp. 310 ff.
Gaye, *J. Phil.* XXXI. 1908, pp. 94–116 (on the "stadium").
Hamelin, *Année Philos.* XVII. 1906, pp. 39 ff. (on the "arrow").
Lachelier, *Rev. Mét. et Mor.* XVIII. 1910, pp. 345 ff. (on the "arrow" and the "stadium").
Milhaud, *Les Philosophes-Géomètres de la Grèce, Platon et ses prédécesseurs* (Paris, 1908), pp. 130 ff.; *Rev. Mét. et Mor.* I. 1893, pp. 150–6, 400–6.
Tannery, *Pour l'histoire de la Science Hellène* (2me éd. Paris, 1930), pp. 255–70; *Rev. Phil.* XX. 1885, pp. 385–97.
Wicksteed and Cornford, *Aristotle, Physics*, vol. II (Loeb ed.).
Zeller, *Phil. der Griechen*, I. I, ed. 6, pp. 755–65; Eng. trans. *Pre-Socratic Philosophy*, by S. F. Alleyne, 1881, vol. I. pp. 608 ff.

Reference may also be made to Prof. A. E. Taylor's essay "Parmenides, Zeno and Socrates" (*Philosophical Studies*, II), and to his *The Parmenides of Plato*, Appendix A.

My thanks are due to Prof. Cornford for lending me the proofs of the Loeb *Physics*, vol. II, and to Dr Ross for the loan of an unpublished paper of his on Zeno's arguments on motion.

given by Diels in his *Vorsokratiker*[1] is adequate, and shall merely give a brief summary.[2]

For the first kind Aristotle and the three commentators Themistius, Simplicius and Philoponus are our chief sources. I have been able to find hardly any relevant information elsewhere, as e.g. in the doxographers.[3] My quotations from Aristotle and the commentators I have tried to make exhaustive, though certain passages which clearly add nothing to our knowledge I have omitted.

Of the three commentators Themistius, though the earliest in date, is admittedly little more than paraphrase, and Philoponus is latest in date and very uninspired. Simplicius is by far the best of the three, and definitely claims (*Physics*, 140. 27) to have had access to an original work of Zeno. Whether this work was genuine or not,[4] it at any rate represents a source of information independent of Aristotle. But Simplicius actually quotes only from the arguments on plurality, and makes no reference to Zeno's work in his exposition of the four arguments on motion; and had his original contained them this

---

[1] Referred to simply as Diels, and quoted by section (e.g. 19. A. 1). My references are to his 4th ed. The 5th ed., now in course of publication, reprints the text of the 4th ed. without alteration. The only change is that, whereas in the 4th ed. the chapter of passages from Zeno is numbered 19, in the 5th ed. it is numbered 29.

[2] See under "Life and Writings" below.

[3] Proclus's commentary on the first part of the *Parmenides* does not seem to me to throw any fresh light on Zeno. Certainly I can find nothing quotable as giving Zeno's authentic doctrine. And the fragments of Melissos, Arist. *M.X.G.*, and Gorgias in Sextus, *adv. Math.* seem similarly devoid of any direct reference to Zeno. They would of course be relevant to a consideration of the influence of Zeno on Greek thought (cf. Conclusion, pp. 109 ff.): but they do not seem to me to have any value for establishing directly what Zeno actually said.

[4] Tannery, *Rev. Phil.* xx. 1885, p. 391, thinks Simplicius "ne possédait qu'un résumé". Zeller (English ed. 1891), p. 611 note, thinks Simplicius "had probably something more than extracts", though not a complete text.

omission is remarkable in view of their admitted difficulty. Nor do I think his exposition implies any knowledge of the arguments apart from what he knew from Aristotle, and, possibly, commentaries on him. In other words, the first-hand information he claims covers only the arguments on plurality, not those on motion. Themistius and Philoponus show no signs of having had first-hand knowledge.

In my collection I have quoted first Simplicius, as his commentary is the best and most informative, next the other commentator, Philoponus, and finally Themistius' paraphrase.

TEXT

For the commentators I have followed the text of the Berlin edition;[1] for the two fragments from the doxographers (17 and 18) that of Diels' *Doxographi Graeci*. In the remaining passages, those quoted from Aristotle, I have, except in two instances, printed Bekker's text. The exceptions are Nos. 29 and 35, which deal with the last two arguments on motion, the "arrow" and the "stadium". Here the text presents considerable difficulties; and I have attempted to explain in my notes to the two passages the readings which I think should be adopted.

LIFE & WRITINGS

(a) LIFE

Zeno's *floruit* is round about the middle of the fifth century. Apollodorus gives it as Ol. LXXIX (464–460 B.C.). On the other hand in the *Parmenides* he is supposed to be "about 40" (127 *b* ἐγγὺς τῶν τετταράκοντα); and the dramatic date of that

---

[1] To which I refer by page and line, e.g. 140. 21 means page 140, line 21.

dialogue is 451–449 B.C. (cf. *E.G.P.*³ p. 169), which gives us a *floruit* about ten years later than that given by Apollodorus. This later date is probably to be accepted. For Plato is very circumstantial and detailed in his account of the relative ages of the chief characters of the *Parmenides*. Parmenides is sixty-five, Zeno is forty, and Socrates a "very young man" (σφόδρα νέον 127 *b*). And it seems unlikely that Plato would have been so precise entirely without reason. Besides, this is the kind of factual detail in which the dialogues are generally admitted to be trustworthy: it is in the opinions he attributes to his characters rather than in detailed matters of fact that Plato is generally supposed not to be strictly historical. The full discussion of the point would necessitate a consideration of the historicity of the Platonic dialogues in general; it is enough here merely to have indicated the reasons in favour of the acceptance of Plato's dating.

We may therefore suppose that Zeno was forty years of age about the year 450 B.C. But apart from this we have practically no information about the detailed events of his life. Tradition is unanimous that he was a disciple and follower of Parmenides (Diels, 19. A. *passim*).¹ It is to be presumed that he spent a large part of his life in his native Elea. At any rate Diogenes says of him that he was ὑπεροπτικὸς τῶν μειζόνων and preferred Elea to Athens, οὐκ ἐπιδημήσας πώμαλα πρὸς αὐτοὺς (sc. τοὺς Ἀθηναίους). On the other hand we have no reason to suppose that he did not visit Athens at some period during his life, as Diogenes implies and Plato states in the *Parmenides*. He is said to have been paid good fees at Athens for his instruction ([Plato], *Alcib.* 1. 119 *a*), and we are told that Pericles himself "heard" him (Plut. *Pericl.* 4, 3; Diels, 19. A. 4). But

¹ Diogenes even says his adopted son: but this may well be a misunderstanding of a phrase in Plato's *Sophist*, 241 *d*; *E.G.P.*³ p. 311. Zeno's father's name was Teleutagoras, Diels, 19. A. 1.

how long or how frequent Zeno's visits were we cannot say with certainty.[1]

Like other early philosophers he was neither a studious recluse nor a man of purely academic interests, but took an active part in the politics of his native city (cf. Diels, 19. A. 1; 18. A. 12). He is traditionally supposed to have been put to death for conspiring against a tyrant, and variant versions of his heroism under torture are given (Diels, 19. A. 1, 2, 6, 8, 9). When his death took place we cannot say: but it is a not unlikely inference from the stories of his execution that he did not live to any very great age. Perhaps 430 B.C. may be suggested as a *terminus ante quem*.

(b) WRITINGS

By far the most important evidence about the nature and purpose of Zeno's writings is that of Plato, *Parmenides*, 127–8.

According to this Zeno had, when he was comparatively young (at the time of the dialogue he was, as we have seen, "nearly forty"), written a book, which was published without his consent. His object in it was to support the view of Parmenides, that what is, is one, by taking the opposite view, that what is, is a many, and showing that it leads to conclusions that are equally absurd. And Plato seems to go out of his way to contradict the opinion that Zeno wrote merely in a spirit of

---

[1] Prof. Taylor ("Parmenides, Zeno and Socrates", in his *Philosophical Studies*) thinks that Zeno "must have settled in Athens and practised his calling there for some considerable time" (*op. cit.* p. 37). He bases his statement largely on the passage from the *First Alcibiades* to which I have just referred, and in which we are told that Pythodorus son of Isolochus and Callias son of Calliades, "two well-known public men of the fifth century" (*ibid.*), paid him 100 minae each for his instruction. Prof. Taylor also cites Plutarch's story that Pericles "heard" Zeno. In the *First Alcibiades* we certainly have fourth-century testimony; and, if this testimony is to be relied on, it makes it seem quite likely that Zeno spent some years teaching at Athens.

wanton paradox, and to state emphatically that his book was a perfectly serious philosophical work written in defence of Parmenides and against those who "made fun of him" (κωμῳδεῖν *Parm.* 129 *a*).

This general view of Zeno's writings is repeated in the commentators (cf. Simp. *Phys.* 134. 4, 102. 30; Diels, 19. A. 23; Philop. *Phys.* 42. 9, 80. 23; Diels, 19. A. 21). And though the recurrence of the word κωμῳδεῖν in both Simplicius and Philoponus makes it seem almost certain that Plato was their source, yet at any rate it shows that they knew of no other tradition of the general tenor of Zeno's work; and there seems to be no reason whatever for not accepting theirs and Plato's opinion.

In form Zeno's work seems to have consisted of more than one λόγος (*Parm.* 127*d*; according to Proclus there were forty: Diels, 19. A. 15); "and these discourses were subdivided into sections dealing with some one presupposition of his adversaries" (*E.G.P.*[3] pp. 312–13). In other words Zeno's method was to start from some premiss or principle admitted by his opponents and to deduce from it absurd or contradictory conclusions. And so we can understand why Aristotle called Zeno the founder of dialectic (Diels, 19. A. 1; Suidas repeats the statement, Diels, 19. A. 2). For part of the definition of dialectic according to Aristotle is that it consists in arguing from premisses whose truth is more or less widely assumed, from ἔνδοξα (*Top.* A. 1),[1] and it was ἔνδοξα on the subject of motion and plurality in particular that Zeno was concerned to discredit by taking them as premisses and showing that the conclusions which they involved are absurd. And if we take, as the definition of dialectic, the drawing of conclusions from

---

[1] Cf. *E.G.P.*[3] p. 314, "dialectic is the art of arguing not from true premisses, but from premisses admitted by the other side".

more or less widely[1] accepted truths, it fits Zeno's procedure very well. Only it must be added that Zeno was concerned to draw conclusions that were self-contradictory.

Suidas gives the titles of four books by Zeno (Diels, 19. A. 2): Ἔριδες, Ἐξήγησις τῶν Ἐμπεδοκλέους, Πρὸς τοὺς Φιλοσόφους, Περὶ Φύσεως. But it is impossible to regard this information with very much confidence. We cannot identify any of the four as the book mentioned by Plato—the Ἔριδες seems the most likely of the four, that is all one can say. The Ἐξήγησις, if genuine, may have been not a commentary on Empedocles but a polemic against him (*E.G.P.*[3] p. 312, note 1). The title Περὶ Φύσεως is quite uninformative: and in any case it is not certain whether it should not be taken with the previous words, and the whole title read Πρὸς τοὺς Φιλοσόφους περὶ Φύσεως.

On the other hand Πρὸς τοὺς Φιλοσόφους seems to ring truer —and if genuine contains definite information. For in the fifth century the word φιλόσοφος had not yet its generalised meaning of "philosopher", but meant Pythagorean. And it seems unlikely that after the fifth century, when the word had so much more generalised a meaning, there could have been any sense in giving a philosophical work this title, which could only have been intelligible as long as the term φιλόσοφος kept its specialised meaning. If this argument is valid, we have in this title evidence that Zeno wrote attacking the Pythagoreans.

(c) CONCLUSIONS

(1) We have every reason to suppose that in his general views Zeno was an orthodox Eleatic.

(2) But he developed a particular type of argument whose object was to show that hypotheses other than the Parmenidean

[1] "more or less widely": cf. Aristotle's definition of ἔνδοξα, 100*b* 21 ἔνδοξα δὲ τὰ δοκοῦντα πᾶσιν ἢ τοῖς πλείστοις ἢ τοῖς σοφοῖς.

"what is, is one" lead to self-contradictory results. His object
was to discredit the pluralists. We should not therefore, for
instance, expect to find that he held any particular views about
the nature of motion, but simply that he tried, as an orthodox
Eleatic, to show that the whole idea of motion is self-contradictory and absurd.

(3) There is some reason to suppose that the Pythagoreans
in particular were the object of his attacks—as indeed they had
been of Parmenides' before him.

TEXT, TRANSLATION, & NOTES

I now go on to give my collection and translation of the
paraphrases and quotations of Zeno's arguments, and to elucidate in a brief commentary some of the more important points
in them. The fragments fall into four obvious classes—those on
plurality, those on motion, the arguments about place or space
(τόπος), and the dilemma of the falling millet-seed which
Simplicius gives in the form of a dialogue between Zeno and
Protagoras. I have accordingly divided the fragments into
these four sections, putting first those dealing with plurality,
second the argument about place, thirdly the arguments on
motion, and lastly the millet-seed puzzle. This main division
is obvious and not likely to be questioned. The more detailed
arrangement of the fragments is bound to be to some extent
arbitrary. The fragments on motion naturally fall into four
sections each concerned with one of the four famous
arguments; but apart from this I have simply followed what
seemed to me a reasonably intelligible order, and in places
have explained my reasons for the particular order adopted.

I. PLURALITY

PLURALITY

§ A. *Arguments directed to prove Eleatic monism*

1. Simplicius, 139. 19

(i) καὶ ὁ Θεμίστιος δὲ τὸν Ζήνωνος λόγον ἓν εἶναι τὸ ὂν κατα-σκευάζειν φησίν, ἐκ τοῦ συνεχές τε αὐτὸ εἶναι καὶ ἀδιαίρετον. "εἰ γὰρ διαιροῖτο, φησίν, οὐδὲ ἔσται ἀκριβῶς ἓν διὰ τὴν ἐπ' ἄπειρον τομὴν τῶν σωμάτων."

5 (ii) Cf. Themistius, f. 12. 1. ⟨Ζήνων⟩ ἐκ τοῦ συνεχές τε εἶναι καὶ ἀδιαίρετον ἓν εἶναι τὸ ὂν κατεσκεύαζε, λέγων ὡς εἰ διαιρεῖται, οὐδὲ ἔσται βεβαίως ἕν, διὰ τὴν ἐπ' ἄπειρον τομὴν τῶν σωμάτων.

2. Simplicius, 139. 27

Attributed by Porphyry to Parmenides: but as Simplicius remarks (140. 21) more likely to be Zeno's.

ἕτερος δὲ ἦν λόγος τῷ Παρμενίδῃ ὁ διὰ τῆς διχοτομίας οἰόμενος δεικνύναι τὸ ὂν ἓν εἶναι μόνον καὶ τοῦτο ἀμερὲς καὶ ἀδιαίρετον.
10 εἰ γὰρ εἴη, φησί, διαιρετόν, τετμήσθω δίχα, ὡς ἤτοι ὑπομένει τινὰ ἔσχατα μεγέθη ἐλάχιστα καὶ ἄτομα, πλήθει δὲ ἄπειρα, καὶ τὸ ὅλον ἐξ ἐλαχίστων, πλήθει δὲ ἀπείρων συστήσεται· ἢ φροῦδον ἔσται καὶ εἰς οὐδὲν ἔτι διαλυθήσεται καὶ ἐκ τοῦ μηδενὸς συστήσεται· ἅπερ ἄτοπα. οὐκ ἄρα διαιρεθήσεται, ἀλλὰ μενεῖ ἕν. καὶ γὰρ δὴ
15 ἐπεὶ πάντῃ ὅμοιόν ἐστιν, εἴπερ διαιρετὸν ὑπάρχει, πάντῃ ὁμοίως ἔσται διαιρετόν, ἀλλ' οὐ τῇ μέν, τῇ δὲ οὔ. διῃρήσθω δὴ πάντῃ· δῆλον οὖν πάλιν ὡς οὐδὲν ὑπομένει, ἀλλ' ἔσται φροῦδον, καὶ εἴπερ συστήσεται, πάλιν ἐκ τοῦ μηδενὸς συστήσεται. εἰ γὰρ ὑπομενεῖ τι, οὐδέ πω γενήσεται πάντῃ διῃρημένον. ὥστε ἐκ τούτων φανε-
20 ρόν φησι, ὡς ἀδιαίρετόν τε καὶ ἀμερὲς καὶ ἓν ἔσται τὸ ὄν.

3. Philoponus, 80. 23

Ζήνων δὲ ὁ τούτου μαθητὴς συνηγορῶν τῷ διδασκάλῳ κατε-σκεύαζεν ὅτι καὶ ἓν τὸ ὂν καὶ ἀκίνητον ἐξ ἀνάγκης, ταῦτα δὲ κατεσκεύαζεν ἐκ τῆς ἐπ' ἄπειρον τῶν συνεχῶν διχοτομίας, εἰ γὰρ

PLURALITY

§ A. *Arguments directed to prove Eleatic monism*

1. Simplicius, 139. 19

(i) And Themistius says that Zeno's argument tries to prove that what is, is one, from its being continuous and indivisible. "For" runs the argument "if it were divided, it would not be one in the strict sense because of the infinite divisibility of bodies."

(ii) Themistius, f. 12. 1. ⟨Zeno⟩ tried to prove that what is, is 5 one, from its being continuous and indivisible, arguing that, if it were divided, it would not be validly one, because of the infinite divisibility of bodies.

2. Simplicius, 139. 27

Parmenides had another argument which was thought to prove by means of dichotomy that what is, is one only, and accordingly 10 without parts and indivisible. For, he argues, if it were divisible, then suppose the process of dichotomy to have taken place: then either there will be left certain ultimate magnitudes, which are minima and indivisible, but infinite in number, and so the whole will be made up of minima but of an infinite number of them; or 15 else it will vanish and be divided away into nothing, and so be made up of parts that are nothing. Both of which conclusions are absurd. It cannot therefore be divided, but remains one. Further, since it is everywhere homogeneous, if it is divisible, it will be divisible everywhere alike, and not divisible at one point and indivisible at another. 20 Suppose it therefore everywhere divided. Then it is clear again that nothing remains and it vanishes, and so that, if it is made up of parts, it is made up of parts that are nothing. For so long as any part having magnitude is left, the process of division is not complete. And so, he argues, it is obvious from these considerations that what 25 is is indivisible, without parts, and one.

3. Philoponus, 80. 23

His disciple Zeno, in support of his master, tried to prove that what is, is of necessity one and unmoved. He rested his proof of this on the infinite divisibility of any continuum. For, he argued, if what is were not one and indivisible, but were divided into a 30

μὴ ἓν εἴη τὸ ὂν καὶ ἀδιαίρετον, ἀλλὰ διαιροῖτο εἰς πλείονα, οὐδὲν
ἔσται κυρίως ἕν (εἰ γὰρ διαιροῖτο τὸ συνεχές, ἐπ' ἄπειρον ἂν εἴη
διαιρετόν), εἰ δὲ μηδέν ἐστι κυρίως ἕν, οὐδὲ πολλά, εἴ γε τὰ πολλὰ
ἐκ πολλῶν ἑνάδων συγκεῖται. ἀδύνατον ἄρα εἰς πολλὰ διαιρεῖσθαι
5 τὸ ὄν· μόνως ἄρα ἕν ἐστιν. ἢ οὕτως· εἰ μὴ τὸ ἓν εἴη, φησί, καὶ
ἀδιαίρετον, οὐδὲ πολλὰ ἔσται· τὰ γὰρ πολλὰ ἐκ πολλῶν ἑνάδων.
ἑκάστη οὖν ἑνὰς ἤτοι μία ἐστὶ καὶ ἀδιαίρετος, ἢ καὶ αὐτὴ εἰς
πολλὰ διαιρεῖται. εἰ μὲν οὖν μία ἐστὶ καὶ ἀδιαίρετος ἑκάστη μονάς,
ἐξ ἀτόμων μεγεθῶν τὸ πᾶν ἔσται, εἰ δὲ καὶ αὗται διαιροῦνται,
10 πάλιν περὶ ἑκάστης τῶν διαιρουμένων μονάδων πευσόμεθα ταὐτά·
καὶ τοῦτο ἐπ' ἄπειρον. ὥστε ἀπειράκις ἄπειρον ἔσται τὸ πᾶν, εἰ
πολλὰ εἴη τὰ ὄντα. εἰ δὲ τοῦτο ἄτοπον, μόνως ἄρα ἓν τὸ ὄν, καὶ
πολλὰ εἶναι τὰ ὄντα οὐχ οἷόν τε· ἑκάστην γὰρ μονάδα ἀπειράκις
τεμεῖν ἀνάγκη, ὅπερ ἄτοπον.

§ B.   *Arguments directed against a plurality of henads*

4. Aristotle, *Met.* B 4. 1001 *b* 7

15 ἔτι εἰ ἀδιαίρετον αὐτὸ τὸ ἕν, κατὰ μὲν τὸ Ζήνωνος ἀξίωμα
οὐθὲν ἂν εἴη. ὃ γὰρ μήτε προστιθέμενον μήτε ἀφαιρούμενον ποιεῖ
μεῖζον μηδὲ ἔλαττον, οὔ φησιν εἶναι τοῦτο τῶν ὄντων, ὡς δηλονότι ὄντος μεγέθους τοῦ ὄντος· καὶ εἰ μέγεθος, σωματικόν· τοῦτο
γὰρ πάντῃ ὄν. τὰ δὲ ἄλλα πῶς μὲν προστιθέμενα ποιήσει μεῖζον,
20 πῶς δ' οὐθέν, οἷον ἐπίπεδον καὶ γραμμή· στιγμὴ δὲ καὶ μονὰς
οὐδαμῶς.

Alexander's comment *ad loc.* amplifies this, but does not add
anything.

5. Simplicius, 97. 13 (same quotation at 138. 32)

Quoting Eudemus: καὶ Ζήνωνά φασι λέγειν, εἴ τις αὐτῷ τὸ ἓν
ἀποδοίη τί ποτέ ἐστι, ἕξειν τὰ ὄντα λέγειν. ἠπόρει δὲ ὡς ἔοικε
διὰ τὸ τῶν μὲν αἰσθητῶν ἕκαστον κατηγορικῶς τε πολλὰ λέγεσθαι
25 καὶ μερισμῷ, τὴν δὲ στιγμὴν μηδὲ ἕν[1] τιθέναι· ὁ γὰρ μήτε προστιθέμενον αὔξει μήτε ἀφαιρούμενον μειοῖ, οὐκ ᾤετο τῶν ὄντων
εἶναι.

[1] 139. 1 μηθέν.

plurality, nothing would be one in the proper sense (for, if the continuum were divided, it would be divisible *ad infinitum*); but, if nothing is one in the proper sense, there can be no plurality, if plurality consists of a plurality of units. It is therefore impossible for what is to be divided into a plurality: it is therefore one only. 5 Alternatively the argument may run as follows. If there were no indivisible unit, there could be no plurality, for plurality consists of a plurality of units. Each unit then is either one and indivisible, or itself divided into a plurality. Therefore, if each unit is one and indivisible, the whole is built up of indivisible magnitudes; but, if 10 the units are themselves divided, we shall again ask the same question about each of these units that are so divided, and so on *ad infinitum*. And so the whole will be infinitely many times infinite, if there is a plurality of things that are. But, if this is absurd, then what is, is one only, and it is not possible for there to be a plurality of things 15 that are: for it is necessary to divide each unit an infinite number of times, which is absurd.

§ B. *Arguments directed against a plurality of henads*

4. Aristotle, *Met.* B 4. 1001 *b* 7

Further, if unity-itself is indivisible, it will according to Zeno's principle be nothing. For what does not make greater when added nor smaller when subtracted he denies to have existence at all, on 20 the grounds, clearly, that whatever exists has spatial magnitude. And if it has spatial magnitude it is corporeal; for the corporeal has existence in every dimension. But the other ⟨objects of mathematics⟩, that is plane and line, will make greater if added in one way, but not if added in another: while point and unit do so in no way whatever. 25

5. Simplicius, 97. 13 (same quotation at 138. 32)

And they say that Zeno said that, if anyone would explain to him what the one is, he would be able to speak about existent things. He raised the difficulty, it seems, because each particular sensible object is called many both categorically and by division, but the point he supposed to be nothing at all. For what does not increase 30 a thing when added to it, nor decrease it when subtracted from it, he thought has no existence.

6. Simplicius, 99. 7

ἐν ᾗ ὁ μὲν Ζήνωνος λόγος ἄλλος τις ἔοικεν οὗτος εἶναι παρ'
ἐκεῖνον τὸν ἐν βιβλίῳ φερόμενον, οὗ καὶ ὁ Πλάτων ἐν τῷ Παρμενίδῃ μέμνηται. ἐκεῖ μὲν γὰρ ὅτι πολλὰ οὐκ ἔστι δείκνυσι
βοηθῶν ἐκ τοῦ ἀντικειμένου τῷ Παρμενίδῃ ἓν εἶναι λέγοντι·
5 ἐνταῦθα δέ, ὡς ὁ Εὔδημός φησι, καὶ ἀνῄρει τὸ ἕν (τὴν γὰρ στιγμὴν
ὡς τὸ ἓν λέγει), τὰ δὲ πολλὰ εἶναι συγχωρεῖ. ὁ μέντοι Ἀλέξανδρος
καὶ ἐνταῦθα τοῦ Ζήνωνος ὡς τὰ πολλὰ ἀναιροῦντος μεμνῆσθαι
τὸν Εὔδημον οἴεται. "ὡς γὰρ ἱστορεῖ, φησίν, Εὔδημος, Ζήνων ὁ
Παρμενίδου γνώριμος ἐπειρᾶτο δεικνύναι, ὅτι μὴ οἷόν τε τὰ ὄντα
10 πολλὰ εἶναι τῷ μηδὲν εἶναι ἐν τοῖς οὖσιν ἕν, τὰ δὲ πολλὰ πλῆθος
εἶναι ἑνάδων."

7. Simplicius, 138. 3 (ad Phys. A 4 187a 1)

τὸν δὲ δεύτερον λόγον τὸν ἐκ τῆς διχοτομίας τοῦ Ζήνωνος
εἶναί φησιν ὁ Ἀλέξανδρος λέγοντος, ὡς εἰ μέγεθος ἔχοι τὸ ὂν καὶ
διαιροῖτο, πολλὰ τὸ ὂν καὶ οὐχ ἓν ἔτι ἔσεσθαι, καὶ διὰ τούτου
15 δείκνυντος ὅτι μηδὲν τῶν ὄντων ἔστι τὸ ἕν.

8. Philoponus, Phys. 42. 9; Diels, A 21

Ζήνων γὰρ ὁ Ἐλεάτης πρὸς τοὺς διακωμῳδοῦντας τὴν Παρμενίδου τοῦ διδασκάλου αὐτοῦ δόξαν λέγουσαν ἓν τὸ ὂν εἶναι ἐνιστά-
μενος καὶ συνηγορῶν τῇ τοῦ διδασκάλου δόξῃ, ἐπεχείρει δεικνύναι
ὅτι ἀδύνατον πλῆθος εἶναι ἐν τοῖς οὖσι. εἰ γάρ, φησίν, ἔστι πλῆθος,
20 ἐπειδὴ τὸ πλῆθος ἐκ πλειόνων ἑνάδων συγκεῖται, ἀνάγκη εἶναι
ἑνάδας πλείους ἐξ ὧν τὸ πλῆθος συνέστηκεν. εἰ τοίνυν δείξομεν
ὅτι ἀδύνατον εἶναι πλείονας ἑνάδας, δῆλον ὅτι ἀδύνατον εἶναι
πλῆθος· τὸ γὰρ πλῆθος ἐξ ἑνάδων. εἰ δὲ ἀδύνατον εἶναι πλῆθος,
ἀναγκὴ δὲ ἢ τὸ ἓν εἶναι ἢ τὸ πλῆθος, πλῆθος δὲ εἶναι οὐ δύναται,
25 λείπεται τὸ ἓν εἶναι. πῶς οὖν ἐδείκνυεν ὅτι οὐ δυνατὸν εἶναι
ἑνάδας πλείους; ἐπειδὴ οἱ τὸ πλῆθος εἰσάγοντες ἐκ τῆς ἐναργείας
τοῦτο ἐπιστοῦντο (ἔστι γὰρ ἵππος καὶ ἄνθρωπος καὶ ἕκαστον τῶν
κατὰ μέρος, ὧν ἡ ἄθροισις τὸ πλῆθος ἀποτελεῖ), τὴν ἐνάργειαν
οὖν σοφιστικῶς ἀνασκευάσαι βουλόμενος ὁ Ζήνων ἔλεγεν ὅτι, εἰ
30 ἐκ τούτων τὸ πλῆθος, τὸ δὲ πλῆθος ἐξ ἑνάδων, ταῦτα ἄρα ἑνάδες.
ἐὰν οὖν δείξωμεν ὅτι οὐ δυνατὸν εἶναι ταῦτα ἑνάδας, δῆλον ὅτι

6. Simplicius, 99. 7

Zeno's argument in this passage seems to be different from the one in his book to which Plato refers in the *Parmenides*. For there, arguing in support of Parmenides's monism from the opposite point of view, he shows that there is no plurality: but here, as Eudemus says, he both does away with the one (for he speaks of the point as 5 the one), and allows the existence of plurality. However Alexander thinks that here too Eudemus is referring to Zeno as doing away with plurality. He says: "As Eudemus records, Zeno the friend of Parmenides tried to show that it is not possible for there to be plurality because there is no 'one' among existing things, and plurality 10 is a collection of units."

7. Simplicius, 138. 3 (*ad Phys.* A 4, 187a 1)

Alexander says that the second argument, that from dichotomy, is Zeno's, who says that, if what is had magnitude and were divided, then what is would be a plurality and no longer one, and thus shows that the one is not an existent.   15

8. Philoponus, *Phys.* 42. 9; Diels, A 21

For Zeno the Eleatic opposed those who made fun of his master Parmenides's opinion that what is, is one, and in support of his master's opinion tried to show that there can be no plurality among the things that are. For if, he says, there is a plurality, since a plurality consists of a number of units, it is necessary that there 20 should be a number of units of which the plurality is made up. If therefore we show that it is impossible for there to be a number of units, it is clear that it is impossible for there to be a plurality; for a plurality is made up of units. But, if it is impossible for there to be a plurality, yet it is necessary for there to be either one or a 25 plurality, but it is impossible for there to be a plurality, we are left with the conclusion that there is one. How then did Zeno try to prove that it is not possible for there to be a number of units? Those who introduce plurality put their confidence in its self-evidence; for there exist horses and men and a variety of individual things, 30 and the aggregation of these produces plurality. This self-evidence therefore Zeno attempted to overthrow sophistically, arguing that, if plurality is composed of these things, but plurality is composed of units, then these things must be units. If therefore we show that

οὐδὲ ἔσται τὸ ἐξ αὐτῶν πλῆθος, εἴ γε τὸ πλῆθος ἐξ ἐνάδων.
δείκνυσιν οὖν τοῦτο οὕτως· ὁ Σωκράτης, φησίν, ὃν λέγετε ἐνάδα
εἶναι συντελοῦσαν εἰς τὴν τοῦ πλήθους σύστασιν, οὐ μόνον
Σωκράτης ἐστίν, ἀλλὰ καὶ λευκὸς καὶ φιλόσοφος καὶ προγάστωρ
5 καὶ σιμός· ὥστε ὁ αὐτὸς ἓν καὶ πολλὰ ἔσται. ἀλλὰ μὴν τὸν αὐτὸν
ἕνα εἶναι καὶ πολλὰ ἀδύνατον, οὐκ ἄρα ἔσται ἓν ὁ Σωκράτης.
ὁμοίως οὐδὲ τὰ λοιπὰ ἐξ ὧν τὸ πλῆθος εἶναί φατε. εἰ δὲ μὴ
δυνατὸν εἶναι πλείους ἐνάδας, δῆλον ὅτι οὐδὲ τὸ πλῆθος ἔσται· εἰ
δὲ ἀνάγκη μὲν εἶναι τὸ ὂν ἢ ἓν ἢ πολλά, δέδεικται δὲ ὅτι πολλὰ
10 οὐκ ἔστι τῷ μὴ εἶναι πλείους ἐνάδας, ἀνάγκη ἄρα ἓν εἶναι.
    τὸ αὐτὸ δὲ τοῦτο καὶ ἐκ τοῦ συνεχοῦς δείκνυσι. τὸ γὰρ συνεχὲς
εἴ ἐστιν ἕν, ἐπειδὴ τὸ συνεχὲς ἀεὶ διαιρετόν, ἔστιν ἀεὶ τὸ διαιρεθὲν
εἰς μόρια διελεῖν πλείονα· εἰ δὴ τοῦτο, πολλὰ ἄρα τὸ συνεχές. τὸ
αὐτὸ ἄρα ἓν ἔσται καὶ πολλά, ὅπερ ἀδύνατον. ὥστε οὐκ ἔσται ἕν.
15 εἰ δὲ μηδὲν τῶν συνεχῶν ἕν, ἀνάγκη δὲ εἴπερ ἔσται τὸ πλῆθος ἐξ
ἐνάδων συγκεῖσθαι, ἐπεὶ * * * οὐδ' ἄρα τὸ πλῆθος ἔσται.

(The sense of the last sentence is plain in spite of the lacuna.)

§ C.   *Passages which apparently quote Zeno's actual words*

9. Simplicius, 139. 5; Diels, fr. 2

ἐν μέντοι τῷ συγγράμματι αὐτοῦ πολλὰ ἔχοντι ἐπιχειρήματα
καθ' ἕκαστον δείκνυσι, ὅτι τῷ πολλὰ εἶναι λέγοντι συμβαίνει τὰ
ἐναντία λέγειν. ὧν ἕν ἐστιν ἐπιχείρημα, ἐν ᾧ δείκνυσιν ὅτι εἰ
20 πολλά ἐστι, καὶ μεγάλα ἐστὶ καὶ μικρά· μεγάλα μὲν ὥστε ἄπειρα
τὸ μέγεθος εἶναι μικρὰ δὲ οὕτως ὥστε μηθὲν ἔχειν μέγεθος. ἐν
δὴ τούτῳ δείκνυσι ὅτι οὗ μήτε μέγεθος μήτε πάχος μήτε ὄγκος
μηθείς ἐστιν οὐδ' ἂν εἴη τοῦτο. "εἰ γὰρ ἄλλῳ ὄντι, φησί, προσ-
γένοιτο, οὐδὲν ἂν μεῖζον ποιήσειεν· μεγέθους γὰρ μηδενὸς ὄντος
25 προσγενομένου δέ, οὐδὲν οἷόν τε εἰς μέγεθος ἐπιδοῦναι. καὶ οὕτως
ἂν ἤδη τὸ προσγενόμενον οὐδὲν εἴη. εἰ δὲ ἀπογενομένου τὸ
ἕτερον μηδὲν ἔλαττον ἔσται μηδὲ αὖ προσγενομένου αὐξήσεται,
δῆλον ὅτι τὸ προσγενόμενον οὐδὲν ἦν οὐδὲ τὸ ἀπογενόμενον."

it is not possible for these things to be units, it is evident that what is made up of them will not be a plurality, if plurality consists of units. His proof that this is so runs as follows: "Socrates, whom you say is a unit contributing to the make-up of plurality, is not only Socrates, but also pale, philosophic, pot-bellied and snub- 5 nosed: and so the same man is at once one and many. But it is quite impossible for the same man to be both one and many; therefore Socrates cannot be one. Similarly with the other things of which you say plurality is composed. But, if it is not possible for there to be a number of units, it is evident there will be no plurality either. 10 And if what is must necessarily be either one or a plurality, and it has been demonstrated that it is not a plurality because there is no such thing as a number of units, it must therefore necessarily be one."

He proves the same conclusion also from a consideration of the continuous. For suppose the continuous is one: then, since the 15 continuous is always divisible, it is always possible to divide the products of division into still further subdivisions, and if this is so the continuous will therefore be many. Thus the same thing will be one and many, which is impossible: and so it will not be one. But if nothing continuous is one, and it is necessary that if there is 20 to be a plurality it should be composed of units, then ⟨since it is not possible for there to be a number of units to constitute plurality⟩ plurality will not exist.

§ C. *Passages which apparently quote Zeno's actual words*

9. Simplicius, 139. 5; Diels, fr. 2

In his book, in which many arguments are put forward, he shows in each that a man who says that there is a plurality is stating some- 25 thing self-contradictory. One of these arguments is that in which he shows that, if there is a plurality, things are both large and small, so large as to be infinite in magnitude, so small as to have no magnitude at all. And in this argument he shows that what has neither magnitude nor thickness nor mass does not exist at all. For, 30 he argues, if it were added to something else, it would not increase its size; for a null magnitude is incapable, when added, of yielding an increase in magnitude. And thus it follows that what was added was nothing. But if, when it is subtracted from another thing, that thing is no less; and again, if, when it is added to another thing, that 35 thing does not increase, it is evident that both what was added and what was subtracted were nothing.

10. Simplicius, 140. 34; Diels, fr. 1

τὸ δὲ κατὰ μέγεθος ⟨sc. ἄπειρον ἔδειξε⟩ πρότερον κατὰ τὴν
αὐτὴν ἐπιχείρησιν. προδείξας γὰρ ὅτι "εἰ μὴ ἔχοι μέγεθος τὸ
ὄν, οὐδ' ἂν εἴη," ἐπάγει "εἰ δὲ ἔστιν, ἀνάγκη ἕκαστον μέγεθός τι
ἔχειν καὶ πάχος καὶ ἀπέχειν αὐτοῦ τὸ ἕτερον ἀπὸ τοῦ ἑτέρου.
5 καὶ περὶ τοῦ προύχοντος ὁ αὐτὸς λόγος. καὶ γὰρ ἐκεῖνο ἕξει
μέγεθος καὶ προέξει αὐτοῦ τι. ὅμοιον δὴ τοῦτο ἅπαξ τε εἰπεῖν
καὶ ἀεὶ λέγειν· οὐδὲν γὰρ αὐτοῦ τοιοῦτον ἔσχατον ἔσται οὔτε
ἕτερον πρὸς ἕτερον οὐκ ἔσται. οὕτως εἰ πολλά ἐστι, ἀνάγκη αὐτὰ
μικρά τε εἶναι καὶ μεγάλα· μικρὰ μὲν ὥστε μὴ ἔχειν μέγεθος
10 μεγάλα δὲ ὥστε ἄπειρα εἶναι."

11. Simplicius, 140. 27; Diels, fr. 3

καὶ τί δεῖ πολλὰ λέγειν, ὅτε καὶ ἐν αὐτῷ φέρεται τῷ τοῦ
Ζήνωνος συγγράμματι; πάλιν γὰρ δεικνύς, ὅτι εἰ πολλά ἐστι τὰ
αὐτὰ πεπερασμένα ἐστὶ καὶ ἄπειρα, γράφει ταῦτα κατὰ λέξιν ὁ
Ζήνων· "εἰ πολλά ἐστι ἀνάγκη τοσαῦτα εἶναι ὅσα ἐστὶ καὶ οὔτε
15 πλείονα αὐτῶν οὔτε ἐλάττονα. εἰ δὲ τοσαῦτά ἐστιν ὅσα ἐστί,
πεπερασμένα ἂν εἴη. εἰ πολλά ἐστιν, ἄπειρα τὰ ὄντα ἐστιν· ἀεὶ
γὰρ ἕτερα μεταξὺ τῶν ὄντων ἐστί, καὶ πάλιν ἐκείνων ἕτερα
μεταξύ. καὶ οὕτως ἄπειρα τὰ ὄντα ἐστί." καὶ οὕτως μὲν τὸ κατὰ
τὸ πλῆθος ἄπειρον ἐκ τῆς διχοτομίας ἔδειξε.

12. Plato, *Parm.* 127e 1–4

20 τὸν οὖν Σωκράτη ἀκούσαντα πάλιν τε κελεῦσαι τὴν πρώτην
ὑπόθεσιν τοῦ πρώτου λόγου ἀναγνῶναι, καὶ ἀναγνωθείσης, Πῶς,
φάναι, ὦ Ζήνων, τοῦτο λέγεις; "εἰ πολλά ἐστι τὰ ὄντα ὡς ἄρα
δεῖ αὐτὰ ὅμοιά τε εἶναι καὶ ἀνόμοια, τοῦτο δὲ ἀδύνατον· οὔτε
γὰρ τὰ ἀνόμοια ὅμοια οὔτε τὰ ὅμοια ἀνόμοια οἷόν τε;" οὐχ οὕτω
25 λέγεις;

10. Simplicius, 140. 34; Diels, fr. 1

The infinity of magnitude he showed previously by the same process of reasoning. For, having first shown that "if what is had not magnitude, it would not exist at all", he proceeds: "But, if it is, then each one must necessarily have some magnitude and thickness and must be at a certain distance from another. And the same reasoning holds good of the one beyond: for it also will have magnitude and there will be a successor to it. It is the same to say this once and to say it always: for no such part will be the last nor out of relation to another. So, if there is a plurality, they must be both small and large. So small as to have no magnitude, so large as to be infinite."

11. Simplicius, 140. 27; Diels, fr. 3

There is no need to labour the point; for such an argument is to be found in Zeno's own book. For in his proof that, if there is plurality, the same things are both finite and infinite, Zeno writes the following words: "If things are a plurality, they must be just as many as they are, and neither more nor less. But, if they are as many as they are, they will be finite in number. If things are a plurality, they will be infinite in number. For there will always be others between any of them, and again between these yet others. And so things are infinite in number." Thus he demonstrates numerical infinity by means of the argument from dichotomy.

12. Plato, *Parm.* 127e 1–4

Socrates, when the reading was complete, asked him to read out again the first hypothesis of the first argument: and, when he had done so, asked "What is it you mean by this, Zeno? 'If things are a plurality' you say 'then they must be both like and unlike, but this is impossible. For it is not possible either for the unlike to be like or the like unlike.' Is not this what you say?"

PLURALITY

§ A

I have grouped the first three passages (Nos. 1, 2, 3) together because they are agreed in emphasising the positive side of Zeno's arguments, that is to say they show quite clearly that the conclusion to be drawn from his attack on plurality was not an utter scepticism, but rather a more strongly reinforced belief in the Parmenidean dogma, "what is, is one". The general nature of the three passages may be summed up by saying that in them Zeno uses the infinite divisibility of magnitude to show that pluralism is absurd and self-contradictory, and so concludes that monism must be accepted. And this is precisely the object which, according to Plato, his arguments had. Apart from his arguments against plurality, motion, etc., Zeno had no philosophical opinions other than those of an orthodox Eleaticism.

1. Although it is not easy to see from these two passages taken in isolation precisely what this argument of Zeno was, yet it is clear that he is represented as using the infinite divisibility of body or magnitude to prove that τὸ ὄν must be continuous and indivisible, and so one. Presumably Zeno showed that to suppose τὸ ὄν infinitely divisible leads to absurd results and so concluded that it must be one and indivisible. Such at any rate is the method of argument in the next two fragments, Nos. 2 and 3.

2. This argument was attributed by Porphyry to Parmenides: but I think that Simplicius's suggestion that it is really Zeno's is certainly correct. Simplicius says (140. 21), "it is worth while considering whether this argument really is Parmenides's, and not, as Alexander thinks, Zeno's. For no such arguments are reported in our traditions about Parmenides (ἐν τοῖς Παρμενιδείοις) and the majority of our information (ἡ πλείστη ἱστορία) refers the difficulty from dichotomy to Zeno". Simplicius's arguments here seem to me to be valid: and I have accordingly followed him and Alexander and attributed the argument to Zeno. A further reason for so doing is that in passage No. 3 we find Philoponus attributing to Zeno an argument closely similar to that in the present passage.[1]

[1] And both Simplicius and Philoponus are commenting on the same passage in Aristotle, *Phys.* A 4, 187a 1.

The argument may be roughly summarised as follows:

Presupposition: the process of division is infinite.

Then if we suppose this process to have taken place what results do we get?

(1) Suppose the resulting subdivisions to have magnitude. Then our initial whole will be composed of an infinite number of parts having magnitude (p. 12, ll. 10–12) ⟨which is absurd⟩.

(2) Suppose them to have no magnitude. Then our initial whole will be composed of *nothings*: which is absurd (p. 12, ll. 12–14).

Alternatively:

(1) Suppose the process of division complete, into parts that have no magnitude. Then the consequence in (2) above results (p. 12, ll. 14–18).

(2) Suppose the parts to have magnitude. Then the process of division is not complete (p. 12, ll. 18–19) ⟨since any magnitude is by definition divisible⟩.

p. 12, l. 10. τετμήσθω δίχα. p. 12, l. 16. διῃρήσθω δὴ πάντῃ. The whole point of Zeno's argument lies in these words, i.e. in supposing a magnitude, by definition infinitely *divisible*, to be actually infinitely *divided*. And the essence of Aristotle's answer to Zeno is that infinite divisibility is by definition a *possibility* only. It has therefore no sense to speak e.g. of a line as infinitely divided: only a process with a finite number of steps can be completed, yield a completed result. Zeno assumes the opposite, and therefore concludes that the conception of magnitude against which he is arguing is self-contradictory.

And, since Zeno's method was to start from the assumptions of his adversaries, we must suppose that he is here attacking some system which tacitly assumed both that magnitude (extension) is infinitely divisible and that it is made up of (indivisible) elements. This will become clearer as we proceed.

3. The argument here is similar to that in the last passage. But this passage adds the idea that if there is to be plurality it must be a plurality composed of units (cf. p. 14, ll. 3–4, 6). And the point of the argument is to show that, as the process of division can go on infinitely, we can never arrive at the indivisible units necessary for the composition of a plurality. As in the first two fragments, the conclusion to be drawn is that "what is, is of necessity one and unmoved" (p. 12, l. 22).

p. 14, ll. 2–3. εἰ γάρ...διαιρετόν, i.e. since there is no terminus to the process of division there is nothing κυρίως ἕν, and so no plurality.

p. 14, l. 9. ἐξ ἀτόμων μεγεθῶν. And this is impossible since the process of division has *ex hypothesi* been supposed infinite. Cf. the last phrase of this passage, ἑκάστην γὰρ μονάδα κ.τ.λ.

The arguments in these three passages illustrate well Zeno's "dialectic" method, described by Plato in the *Parmenides*. For in all these three passages Zeno presupposes the infinite divisibility of the continuum. But this presupposition is in flat contradiction to the Eleatic belief that τὸ ὄν is ἕν, συνεχές and ἀδιαίρετον (cf. Parmenides in Ritter and Preller, No. 118). Zeno is, in fact, arguing from the presuppositions of his *opponents*, and refuting those presuppositions by showing that from them absurd and contradictory results follow; and he concludes that τὸ ὄν is συνεχές and ἀδιαίρετον because from the assumption that it is ἐπ' ἄπειρον διαιρετόν absurd results follow. This is precisely the method of argument he is said to have used by Plato.

§ B

In No. 3 we have seen introduced the idea that if there is to be plurality it must be a plurality composed of units; and the characteristic of all the fragments in the present section is that they are all directed to attack a plurality of this kind. I do not wish to imply that the fragments in § A have any other object of attack; No. 3, as we have seen, certainly has not. The difference between § A and § B is one of emphasis. The emphasis in the passages in § A is on the ultimate conclusion, that what is, is one; and because of this emphasis it seemed right to put them first, as giving the ultimate object of Zeno's reasoning.

The precise nature of the plurality attacked in the present section will, I hope, become clear as I proceed.

4. p. 14, l. 15. ἀδιαίρετον. One of the defining characteristics of the point according to Aristotle: e.g. ἀδύνατον ἐξ ἀδιαιρέτων εἶναί τι συνεχές, οἷον γραμμὴν ἐκ στιγμῶν, εἴπερ ἡ γραμμὴ μὲν συνεχές,

ἡ στιγμὴ δὲ ἀδιαίρετον 231a 24: cf. 220a 20 and *Phys.* Z. 1 *passim.*
And the characteristic of not making greater when added nor smaller when subtracted is also a characteristic of the point, as Aristotle says in the last sentence of this passage.

The passage is part of the eleventh ἀπορία of *Met.* B, which asks, are being and unity substances or attributes? And Aristotle's argument in the section of it here quoted is that if αὐτὸ τὸ ἕν is indivisible, i.e. has the characteristics of the point, then, according to Zeno's principle, it cannot be said to exist at all. (Though Aristotle adds, with a characteristic impatience of Zeno's reasoning, ἀλλ'...οὗτος θεωρεῖ φορτικῶς 1001b 14.)

Zeno's argument must have been directed against the supposition that anything having the characteristics of the geometrical point can be the element out of which plurality is constructed: the argument will not otherwise make sense. We shall find further reason, as we proceed, to believe that such a supposition had actually been made.

Zeno's argument, set out in full, would run as follows: Whatever does not increase a thing when added to it nor decrease it when subtracted from it has no magnitude. Whatever has no magnitude does not exist. Therefore your element, supposed to have the characteristics of the point, does not exist.

p. 14, l. 18. σωματικόν, "corporeal", i.e. solid; for σῶμα can mean solid as opposed to plane (ἐπίπεδον) or line (γραμμή). It is ambiguous between a *physical* or a *geometrical* "body". Perhaps "bodily" would suggest the ambiguity better than "corporeal".

p. 14, l. 19. τὰ δὲ ἄλλα, i.e. plane and line. Cf. note in the Oxf. Trans.: "A line added to another at the end makes it longer, but one which lies beside another makes it no broader."

We might translate alternatively: "But, of the other objects of mathematics, while plane and line, etc...., point and unit, etc...."

5. Here as in No. 3 the element is supposed to be the unit, but at the same time is also supposed to have the characteristics of the point. And we have again the same argument as in the last passage.

p. 14, l. 23. ἕξειν τὰ ὄντα λέγειν, i.e. would be able to grant the existence of a plurality of existent things.

p. 14, l. 25. μηδὲ ἕν. This, the reading printed in the Berlin text, does not seem to give very good sense, and I have accordingly

translated as if the reading were μηθέν as in the parallel passage at
139. 1. This gives the meaning which the argument requires.

Brandis conjectures μηδὲ ἕν τι εἶναι, which gives the same
meaning as μηθέν, but a better antithesis.

6. This is Simplicius's comment on No. 5. No. 5 is part of a long
quotation from Eudemus: and No. 6 is Simplicius's comment on the
first part of it, quoted here as No. 5.

p. 16, ll. 2–3. ἐν τῷ Παρμενίδῃ, i.e. Plato, *Parm.* 127–8. Cf.
No. 12, in which I quote from *Parm.* 127e.

p. 16, l. 4. ἐκ τοῦ ἀντικειμένου. Parmenides argued to prove
monism: Zeno attacked plurality.

p. 16, l. 6. τὰ δὲ πολλὰ...ὁ μέντοι Ἀλέξανδρος.... Alexander's
interpretation is certainly the right one here. For it is quite clear
from Simplicius's quotation of Eudemus (quoted as No. 5) that Zeno
can only be said to have "allowed the existence of plurality" in the
sense that he said that *if* anyone could explain to him what τὸ ἕν
was, then he would be able to give an account of plurality.

Simplicius is puzzled because he finds Zeno, an Eleatic, apparently
attacking τὸ ἕν. Accordingly immediately after this passage he goes
on (99. 16) to deny that Eudemus could have meant that Zeno
attacked τὸ ἕν; and at 139. 17 we again find him contradicting
Alexander, whom he has quoted at 138. 29 as saying that Zeno
ἀνῄρει τὸ ἕν. He fails to perceive that there are two senses of τὸ ἕν
in question, and not one only. There is τὸ ἕν in the sense of the
"one being" of Parmenides, which Zeno is certainly not attacking:
and there is τὸ ἕν in the sense of the ultimate element from which
plurality is made up, which is precisely what Zeno is attacking—as
can be seen from the latter part of this fragment. And it is essential
to keep these two senses distinct.

Simplicius perhaps feels the unsatisfactoriness of his own denials
when, at 139. 3, he says καὶ εἰκὸς μὲν ἦν Ζήνωνα ὡς ἐφ' ἑκάτερα
γυμναστικῶς ἐπιχειροῦντα, falling back on the paradoxical nature
of Zeno's arguments in default of an explanation.

p. 16, ll. 5–6. Note the identification of ἡ στιγμή and τὸ ἕν.

7. Simplicius is commenting on the ἔνιοι δὲ ἐνέδοσαν τοῖς
λόγοις ἀμφοτέροις passage, *Phys.* A, 187a 1, and gives this brief
résumé of Zeno's "argument from dichotomy".

Here again we see the necessity of keeping separate the two senses of τὸ ἕν—the Parmenidean "one being" and the element constituting plurality. Zeno is clearly presupposing that if there is plurality it must be composed of "ones" as elements (cf. p. 14, ll. 3–4, 6, No. 3 above): and argues that if there were such "ones", having magnitude (and if they had no magnitude they would not exist: cf. Nos. 4 and 5), each would be not one, but many, since any magnitude is infinitely divisible (cf. p. 14, ll. 13–14, No. 3 *fin.* ἑκάστην γὰρ μονάδα ἀπειράκις τεμεῖν ἀνάγκη, ὅπερ ἄτοπον).

8. The general form of this argument is as follows:

(1) Any plurality is made up of units.

(2) But the conception of a unit is self-contradictory.

(3) There can therefore be no such thing as a "number of units" (πλείους ἑνάδας), i.e. there can be no plurality.

Step (2) is proved in two different ways. (*a*) The second (p. 18, ll. 11–16) is by the argument from the infinite divisibility of the continuum which we have already met. There is a lacuna at the end of it which clearly requires some such sense as "since ⟨the idea of a plurality of units is self-contradictory⟩...etc." to be supplied. Vitelli in the Berlin edition suggests ἐπεὶ ⟨οὐ δυνατὸν εἶναι πλείους ἑνάδας, ἐξ ὧν τὸ πλῆθος ἔσται⟩, which seems adequate. Otherwise the argument calls for no fresh comment. (*b*) The first way (p. 16, l. 28–p. 18, l. 10) calls for more comment. In itself it contains nothing of note. It is simply the familiar argument that a thing cannot at the same time be *one* and yet have *many* predicates. Socrates is not only Socrates, but also pale, philosophic, etc.: cf. *Sophist*, 251a[1] and *Philebus*, 143 for the same argument. In this there is nothing remarkable: what is remarkable is its attribution here to Zeno. For this is the only passage in which an argument of this kind is attributed to him, and we may therefore reasonably question whether it is reliable.

There seem to be two points which might be urged in its favour:

(1) Such an argument naturally would, and did, arise out of Parmenides's philosophy.

(2) Aristotle does in fact refer to it as an Eleatic argument.

[1] Cf. p. 28 below, note 2.

But against these it may be replied that even though the argument arose naturally from Parmenides's philosophy and was used by the Eleatics, this in itself is not sufficient to show that Zeno in particular used it. And Aristotle does keep the argument from dichotomy (admittedly Zeno's) sharply distinct from it (*Phys.* A, 187*a* 1). So neither of these arguments seems to me to have any great weight.

The arguments on the other side are much stronger:

(1) There is the very isolation of the passage. It is, as I have said, the only passage in which such an argument is attributed to Zeno: and I do not think Philoponus is an authority in whom any implicit trust is to be placed. All[1] the other arguments attributed to Zeno contain an infinite regress in some form, which this does not. And therefore in the light of the existing evidence the argument must be pronounced definitely un-Zenonic.

(2) Chronological considerations. Is not this sort of argument a product rather of the latter part of the fifth and of the fourth century? According to Plato, Zeno must have written his book (the only book of which we have any certain information) not later than 465 B.C. For he was forty at the time of the dramatic date of the *Parmenides* (450 B.C.), and says he wrote it when a young man, i.e. surely before he was twenty-five or so. And I think it more probable that these predication difficulties, though they may have arisen out of Zeno's dialectic, were not actually used by him, but were rather typical of later fifth-century eristic. Though Socrates in the *Parmenides* is made to produce this theory of "participation" in answer to Zeno (*Parm.* 129 *a*, *b*), I do not think that this necessarily means that Zeno must have raised difficulties of this kind about predication.[2] It is more likely that the argument was attributed to him by some ancient commentator by a false inference from this passage in the *Parmenides* (esp. 129 *c*).

(3) It may be added that the use of "Socrates" as an illustration in the argument tells against its being Zeno's. Perhaps it was taken from some dialogue in which Zeno was a character: cf. Diels's note to 19. A. 20.

[1] Except those in Nos. 17 and 18.
[2] Gillespie, *Archiv f. Gesch. d. Phil.* N.F. vols. XIX and XX, 1913–14, thinks that in the passage in the *Sophist* (251 *a*, *b*) referred to above Antisthenes is aimed at.

I am accordingly of the opinion that this argument is not Zeno's, and that Philoponus is in error in attributing it to him.

§ C

The fragments in this section all have this in common, that they appear to contain actual quotations of Zeno's words. So Diels quotes Nos. 9, 10 and 11 all as "fragmente" (19. B. 2, 1, 3). I give the same excerpts from Simplicius as he does, but give them in a different order, reversing the positions of his 1 and 2. My reason for this is that the presupposition of the argument in No. 10, i.e. εἰ μὴ ἔχοι μέγεθος τὸ ὄν, οὐδ' ἂν εἴη, is proved in No. 9: and hence it seemed more natural to quote them in the order given.[1] Diels does not give under "fragmente" the quotation from the *Parmenides* given as No. 12. But Plato appears in it to be quoting, or at least paraphrasing extremely closely, Zeno's own words, and I have accordingly inserted it here.

9. p. 18, ll. 19–21. ὧν ἕν...ἔχειν μέγεθος. This seems to refer briefly to the argument of No. 10 below.

p. 19, l. 32. "null magnitude", lit. a magnitude which is nothing: referring back to "what has neither magnitude nor thickness nor mass".

Zeno argues that such a null magnitude is incapable of increasing anything when added to it or of decreasing it when subtracted from it, and therefore cannot be properly said to be anything, i.e. to exist, at all.

We have already met this argument in Nos. 4 and 5 and noted that this characteristic of neither increasing when added nor decreasing when subtracted is a characteristic of the geometrical point, with which it is explicitly connected by Aristotle in No. 4.

10. The opening words of No. 9 have already referred forward to the argument of this fragment. None the less, since the main argument of No. 9 is concerned to prove the presupposition of this argument, i.e. εἰ μὴ ἔχοι μέγεθος τὸ ὄν, οὐδ' ἂν εἴη, I have preferred to quote No. 9 first.

p. 20, ll. 2–3. εἰ μὴ ἔχοι μέγεθος τὸ ὄν, οὐδ' ἂν εἴη. Proved in No. 9 as we have seen. Zeno assumes it here and then goes on to

[1] Cf. also first note to No. 10.

ask what results if the elements constituting plurality *are* supposed to have magnitude.

p. 20, ll. 7–8. οὔτε ἕτερον πρὸς ἕτερον οὐκ ἔσται, "nor out of relation to another", i.e. the relation described in the previous lines, p. 20, l. 4 καὶ ἀπέχειν . . . p. 20, l. 6 αὐτοῦ τι. For the precise nature of this relation *v.* below on p. 20, l. 10.

p. 20, l. 9. μικρά, because an infinite number of magnitudes cannot make up a finite magnitude: and so we must suppose they have no magnitude. But *v.* following note.

p. 20, l. 10. μεγάλα δὲ ὥστε ἄπειρα εἶναι, "so large as to be infinite". The phrase is ambiguous. Does it mean "so as to be infinite *in number*"? For they certainly are infinite in number, as the infinite regress (ὅμοιον δὴ τοῦτο ἅπαξ τε εἰπεῖν καὶ ἀεὶ λέγειν) proves. But this does not give a good antithesis to μικρὰ ὥστε μὴ ἔχειν μέγεθος: the antithesis should be entirely concerned with magnitude, just as the antithesis in No. 11 is entirely concerned with number (so Simplicius (p. 20, l. 16), referring to his argument, has ἄπειρα τὸ μέγεθος).

The antithesis intended is therefore probably the following: An infinite number of magnitudes cannot make up a finite magnitude. So we must suppose "them" to have no magnitude. But an infinite number of null magnitudes can only make up a null magnitude (p. 20, ll. 2–3).

On the other hand since we have *ex hypothesi* supposed "them" to have magnitude, and since we can prove "them" infinite in number, "they" must make up an infinite magnitude (p. 20, ll. 2–10).

The "they" referred to are of course the elements constituting plurality. But why should Zeno suppose that there is an infinite regress necessarily involved in the hypothesis that plurality is composed of a number of units having magnitude? For in any ordinary atomic hypothesis no such infinite regress is involved. We can only make sense of Zeno's argument by supposing that the elements in question, though assumed to have magnitude, are *also assumed to have the characteristics of the geometrical point*. For a line is divisible infinitely, i.e. is divisible at an infinite number of points, and so we may say that there are an infinite number of points in a line. If we now assume that the line is *made up of* these points we do get Zeno's paradoxical results. Hence we can only make sense of Zeno's argument by assuming that the elements in question are supposed to have the characteristics of the geometrical point, besides having magnitude.

We can now also see more precisely what is the relation described in p. 20, ll. 5 ff. above. It is clearly some relation between points on a line such that the series of points generated is an infinite series. And the infinite divisibility of the line easily gives us such a relation:

$$X \vdash \underset{a}{\rule{0pt}{0pt}} \quad \underset{a^1}{\rule{0pt}{0pt}} \underset{a^2}{\rule{0pt}{0pt}} \underset{a^3}{\rule{0pt}{0pt}} Y$$

If we bisect the line XY at a, and the resultant line aY at a^1 and so on we get a series in which there is always a point "beyond" any given point. A series which fits very well Zeno's, description that "each one has a successor". And I think it was certainly of this serial relation that he was thinking.

11. καὶ τί δεῖ.... These opening words refer to Simplicius's suggestion that the argument quoted as No. 2 above is Zeno's, and not Parmenides's as Porphyry had said (v. note ad loc.). Simplicius clinches his argument by quoting this argument from Zeno's own book as being sufficiently similar to the argument in question to justify him attributing it to Zeno.

Zeno here is arguing that if there is plurality then things must be both finite and infinite in number (as No. 10 was concerned with magnitude, so No. 11 is concerned with number). In the *first* part of his argument he says that any plurality of things must consist of a *definite number* of things and so be finite in number. The *second* part must again make nonsense unless it is understood that the "things" in question are supposed to have the properties of points on a line. And the argument is simply that between any two points a and a^1 it is possible to take further points a^2 and a^3 and so on.

The fragment is interesting because it gives a Zenonian dilemma in the form in which he actually stated it.

12. I have given above my reasons for including this passage here. Plato quotes only the statement of the antinomy; and it is impossible to be sure what Zeno's argument was, or what the exact meaning of ὅμοια and ἀνόμοια is in this context.

For the argument cf. Plato, *Parm.* 139e 7 ff. and 147c 1 ff., where the antithesis ὅμοιον)(ἀνόμοιον is dealt with. The antinomies in the second half of the *Parmenides* are certainly in form an "imitation of the Zenonian method".[1] But lack of evidence makes it difficult to say how far, if at all, their substance is borrowed from Zeno; and so it is not possible to say whether the meaning Plato gives to ὅμοιον in the two passages cited, i.e. τὸ ταὐτὸν πεπονθός, is Zeno's or not. But the definition has a distinctly Platonic ring, and, in my opinion, is definitely not Zeno's. Certainly the term does not bear this meaning in Parmenides and Melissos (R.P. Nos. 118, 145), where it means "homogeneous", "uniform throughout".

But this last meaning is hardly appropriate here, where Zeno is talking about πολλά. One would rather expect some reference to *number*: i.e. that ὅμοια and ἀνόμοια are to be translated "like and unlike *in number*". Even so it is not easy to see what Zeno's argument can have been. I would suggest some argument of which the first step was similar to the first step in No. 11, "if things are a plurality, they must be just as many as they are", while the second step went on to show that "things are also *not* just as many as they are". This might be not unnaturally described as proving that "things are both like and unlike in number". But I cannot say I feel entirely confident about this suggestion.

In this context Plato's reference to the "Eleatic Palamedes", i.e. Zeno, in *Phaedrus*, 261d may be cited: τὸν οὖν Ἐλεατικὸν Παλα-μήδην λέγοντα οὐκ ἴσμεν τέχνῃ, ὥστε φαίνεσθαι τοῖς ἀκούουσι τὰ αὐτὰ ὅμοια καὶ ἀνόμοια, καὶ ἓν καὶ πολλά, μένοντά τε αὖ καὶ φερόμενα. Here the first pair of opposites is the same as that in the present passage just dealt with. The second pair refers no doubt to Zeno's arguments about the one and the many in general, the third to his arguments on motion.

I will now summarise the results that have emerged from this examination of Zeno's arguments on plurality.

(1) From the apophthegm εἴ τις αὐτῷ τὸ ἓν ἀποδοίη τί ποτέ ἐστι, ἕξειν τὰ ὄντα λέγειν (5 init.), and from the argument of Nos. 5, 6 and 8 generally it seems clear (a) that Zeno was attacking a certain conception of τὸ ἕν, (b) that the ἕν in question was the element from which plurality (τὰ πολλά) is constituted.

[1] Taylor, *Plato, the man and his work*, p. 350.

(2) The nett result of Nos. 4, 5, 9 and 10 is, that the element in question cannot without contradiction be supposed to have magnitude, while if it has no magnitude it cannot be an element. From which it is natural to conclude that this element had been supposed to have both magnitude and certain other characteristics which Zeno shows as a matter of fact to be incompatible with its having magnitude.

(3) From No. 4 in particular, from No. 5 and from the phrase τὴν γὰρ στιγμὴν ὡς τὸ ἕν λέγει in No. 6 we may conclude that the unit-element (ἕν) was supposed to have the properties of the geometrical point.

(4) It is absolutely impossible to make any sense of No. 10 unless we suppose that the elements supposed to have μέγεθος have the properties of the point. And the same is true of the second part of the argument in No. 11.

(5) It is clear also that the arguments from the infinite divisibility of the continuum in Nos. 1, 2 and 3 also derive their force from the supposition that the element ultimately to be reached has the properties of the point.

(6) We have seen already that this point-element is the unit from which plurality is constituted. And from the frequent references to it as a "unit" or a "one" it is clear that the point-element had also certain of the characteristics of the numerical unit.

We may therefore give the following account of the system against which Zeno directed his paradoxes; for it seems reasonable to suppose that he was attacking some system or systems, both from the polemical nature of his arguments, and from the explicit testimony of Plato, and if we can reconstruct any single system from the fragments of Zeno's polemic we shall be justified in supposing that this was the system he was attacking. The following, then, seems to be a reasonable reconstruction: Zeno's arguments are directed against a view which supposed (1) that just as repeated additions of the unit make up the series of numbers, so the line may be regarded as made up by repeated additions of point to point. The point is thus supposed to have certain of the characteristics of the unit. (Could we say that the point is the unit spatialised? or would it be truer to say that the two conceptions were not yet clearly differentiated?) (2) As this unit-point is the element from which the line is constructed it must clearly have extension. (3) But it is clearly not simply thought to be extended two-dimensionally. The point-unit is definitely thought to be the atom or element out of which plurality is built up.

In brief, Zeno is attacking a system which made the fundamental error of identifying or at any rate confusing the characteristics of point, unit and atom. And against it his attack is perfectly valid. He produces his contradictions by playing off the contradictory characteristics of point and unit-atom against each other and showing them incompatible. The number of *points* obtainable by division is infinite: the *unit of extension* is an indivisible component. In other words there are implied in the confusion of the attributes of point, unit and atom the contradictory assumptions of infinite divisibility and of the existence of indivisibles.

This conclusion is not new. Milhaud (*Phil.-géomètres*) and Tannery (*Science Hellène* and *Rev. Phil.* xx. pp. 385 ff.) have already argued that Zeno was attacking the Pythagorean μονὰς θέσιν ἔχουσα; and Prof. Cornford (*C.Q.* vols. xvi and xvii) has distinguished the development of Pythagoreanism in question by the name of "number-atomism". I can only claim to have reinforced their conclusion by a rather more detailed study of the evidence.

I will conclude this section of my notes with a quotation from Tannery (*Rev. Phil. loc. cit.* p. 388): "La clef du point faible reconnu par Zénon dans les doctrines pythagoriciennes de son temps, nous est d'ailleurs donnée par leur célèbre définition du point mathématique, définition encore classique au temps d'Aristote.... Le point est l'unité ayant une position (μονὰς ἔχουσα θέσιν), ou l'unité considérée dans l'espace. Il suit immédiatement de cette définition que le corps géométrique est une somme de points, de même que le nombre est une somme d'unités.... D'ailleurs, à cette époque, aucune distinction ne pouvait encore exister entre un corps géométrique et un corps physique; les pythagoriciens se représentaient donc les corps de la nature comme formés par l'assemblage de points physiques."

II. PLACE

PLACE

13. Aristotle, *Phys.* Δ 2. 209 a 23; Diels, A 24

ἔτι δὲ καὶ αὐτὸς ⟨sc. ὁ τόπος⟩ εἰ ἔστι τι τῶν ὄντων, ποῦ
ἔσται; ἡ γὰρ Ζήνωνος ἀπορία ζητεῖ τινα λόγον· εἰ γὰρ πᾶν τὸ
ὂν ἐν τόπῳ, δῆλον ὅτι καὶ τοῦ τόπου τόπος ἔσται, καὶ τοῦτο εἰς
ἄπειρον πρόεισι.

14. Aristotle, *Phys.* Δ 3. 210 b 23; Diels, A 24

5   ὁ δὲ Ζήνων ἠπόρει, ὅτι εἰ ἔστι τι ὁ τόπος, ἐν τίνι ἔσται;
λύειν οὐ χαλεπόν.

15. Simplicius 562. 1, *ad* 210 b 23; Diels, A 24

ὁ Ζήνωνος λόγος ἀναιρεῖν ἐδόκει τὸ εἶναι τὸν τόπον ἐρωτῶν
οὕτως· εἰ ἔστιν ὁ τόπος, ἐν τίνι ἔσται;[1] πᾶν γὰρ ὂν ἔν τινι· τὸ
δὲ ἔν τινι καὶ ἐν τόπῳ. ἔσται ἄρα ὁ τόπος ἐν τόπῳ καὶ τοῦτο
10 ἐπ᾽ ἄπειρον· οὐκ ἄρα ἔστιν ὁ τόπος. 563. 25 *ad ibid.* ὁ Εὔδημος
δὲ οὕτως ἱστορεῖ τὴν Ζήνωνος δόξαν λέγων· "ἐπὶ ταὐτὸ δὲ καὶ ἡ
Ζήνωνος ἀπορία φαίνεται ἄγειν. ἄξιον[2] γὰρ πᾶν τὸ ὂν που εἶναι·
εἰ δὲ ὁ τόπος τῶν ὄντων, ποῦ ἂν εἴη; οὐκοῦν ἐν ἄλλῳ τόπῳ,
κἀκεῖνος δὴ ἐν ἄλλῳ καὶ οὕτως εἰς τὸ πρόσω."

16. Philoponus, 510. 2, *ad* 209 a 23

15   ἔπειτα, φησί, καὶ ἡ Ζήνωνος ἀπορία ζητεῖ τινα λόγον καὶ
ἀπολογίαν· εἰ γὰρ πάντα τὰ ὄντα ἐν τόπῳ, ὡς ἐδόκει τισίν, ἔστι
δὲ καὶ ὁ τόπος τῶν ὄντων, καὶ ὁ τόπος ἄρα ἐν τόπῳ ἔσται, καὶ
πάλιν ἐκεῖνος ἐν ἄλλῳ, καὶ τοῦτο ἐπ᾽ ἄπειρον. Cf. 599. 1 "εἰ γὰρ
πᾶν τὸ ὂν που ἐστιν," ἔλεγεν οὗτος ⟨sc. Ζήνων⟩, "ἔστι δέ τι καὶ
20 ὁ τόπος, καὶ ὁ τόπος ἄρα που ἔσται· ὥστε ἔσται τόπος ἐν τόπῳ,
καὶ τοῦτο ἐπ᾽ ἄπειρον."

Similar forms of the argument are given by Philoponus at 513.
5, 535. 31 and 538. 20. (The differences are not sufficiently great to
justify the quotation of all five.)

25   Themistius's paraphrase of this argument, 105. 12 and 110. 23,
adds nothing to our knowledge.

---

[1] ἔν τινι ἔσται· is the reading in the Berlin text. I have altered this
to agree with Aristotle's ἐν τίνι in l. 5 (cf. also the ποῦ in ll. 1 and 13);
Simplicius' ἐρωτῶν l. 7 also seems to require it.

[2] So the Berlin text. ἀξιοῖ Spengel, Zeller, Diels's *Vors.* Trans. "he
postulates…".

PLACE

13. Aristotle, *Phys.* Δ 2. 209*a* 23; Diels, A 24

Further if ⟨place⟩ is itself an existent, where will it be? For Zeno's difficulty demands some explanation: for if everything that exists has a place, it is clear that place too will have a place and so on *ad infinitum*.

14. Aristotle, *Phys.* Δ 3. 210*b* 23; Diels, A 24

Zeno's difficulty, "if place is something, in what will it be?" is 5 not difficult to solve.

15. Simplicius, 562. 1, *ad* 210*b* 23; Diels, A 24

Zeno's argument seemed to do away with place, putting the question as follows: if place exists, in what will it be? For every existent is in something; but what is in something is in a place. Place therefore will be in a place, and so on *ad infinitum*: therefore 10 place does not exist. 563. 25 *ad ibid.* Eudemus records Zeno's opinion in the following words: "Zeno's difficulty appears to lead to the same conclusion. For it is justifiable to assume that everything that exists is somewhere; but if place exists, where would it be? Presumably in another place, and that in another and so on." 15

16. Philoponus, 510. 2, *ad* 209*a* 23

He goes on to say that Zeno's difficulty demands some explanation and counter-argument. For if everything that exists is in a place, as some supposed, and place is an existent, place also will be in a place, and that again in another and so on *ad infinitum*. Cf. 599. 1 "For if everything that exists is somewhere", said Zeno, "and place 20 exists, place also will be somewhere. And so place will be in a place and so on *ad infinitum*."

PLACE

The Greek τόπος is ambiguous between "place" and "space". In *Phys.* Δ it certainly seems to mean "place" rather than "space": and as Aristotle quotes Zeno's argument in this context I have translated it "place" here.

My justification for putting these fragments between those on plurality and on motion is that there are two isolated fragments (quoted at the beginning of the next main section, on Motion) in which place and motion are connected; and it seemed best to put first the argument about place in general, then the argument about place and its connexion with motion in particular, and finally the four arguments on motion.

The argument in all these passages, Nos. 13, 14, 15, 16, is the same, and needs no comment or explanation. Everything that exists is in a place: place is an existent: therefore place is in a place, and so on *ad infinitum*: which is absurd: οὐκ ἄρα ἔστιν ὁ τόπος. Such is its general form. As to its purpose, Philoponus is probably right when he says (513. 8) that clearly by showing the conception of place self-contradictory Zeno would *a fortiori* be making a pluralistic position untenable. We can thus see a connexion between this argument and his attack on pluralism. But whether it was directed against the Pythagoreans it is impossible to say. For in such a very general argument in itself there is nothing to show whether it did in fact form part of a polemic against a particular school.

There is an argument in Plato, *Parm.* 138 a, b, Sextus, *Adv. Math.* VII. 69, 70 (Diels, 76. A. 3) and *M.X.G.* 979a 22 (the latter two of which passages are accounts of the arguments of Gorgias in his Περὶ Φύσεως ἢ τοῦ μὴ ὄντος) which has much in common with this argument of Zeno on place. τὸ ὄν (in Plato τὸ ἕν) is supposed to be ἄπειρον, and the argument proceeds to show that what is ἄπειρον cannot *be* anywhere, in any place. It runs as follows:

(1) What *is* must *be* somewhere, i.e. in something.

(2) What is ἄπειρον cannot be in something *other than itself*, for then it would not be ἄπειρον.

(3) It cannot be *in itself* (ἐν αὑτῷ) because then τὸ ἐνόν and τὸ ἐν ᾧ, which are *two*, would be one and the same, which is impossible.

Step (1) is only explicitly stated in the *M.X.G.*, where it is expressly attributed to Zeno (μηδαμοῦ δὲ ὂν οὐδὲ εἶναι κατὰ τὸν τοῦ Ζήνωνος λόγον 979 b 25), but is clearly a necessary presupposition of the argument, even if not explicitly stated; for both steps (2) and (3) clearly turn on the assumption, made by Zeno, that τόπος, because it *is*, must be *somewhere* (cf. also Zeno's argument on place and motion, Nos. 17 and 18 below).

I should say therefore that the argument undoubtedly takes its origin from Zeno. But I doubt if its present form and application was due to him. We have no arguments of Zeno that are not an *attack* on other people's views; and the evidence that Zeno's work was entirely polemical is overwhelming. It is conceivable that in some polemic the argument that "τὸ ἄπειρον is nowhere" might occur as a *reductio ad absurdum* of the belief in anything ἄπειρον (cf. the Pythagorean "boundless Breath"); and I do not think that it is at all impossible that Zeno made this use of the argument. But it is used here to prove that τὸ ἓν ὄν, being ἄπειρον, is nowhere; and this direct type of proof about τὸ ὄν is unlike Zeno. Nor do I think it typically Eleatic. We do find arguments in Melissus to show that τὸ ἕν is ἄπειρον and that it cannot move because it has nowhere to move to (cf. *E.G.P.*³ p. 322, frs. (3), (4), (7); R.P. Nos. 143, 145). But Melissus's point is that what is is homogeneously distributed throughout all space (cf. Parmenides, R.P. No. 118); it cannot move anywhere because it already is everywhere. Our argument does not prove this, but rather the opposite conclusion that it cannot *be* at all since it *is* nowhere—a quite un-Eleatic conclusion.

I am accordingly inclined to suppose that the argument in its present form is due to Gorgias, to whom both Sextus and *M.X.G.* attribute it; though Gorgias may be merely adapting for his own purposes an argument of Zeno's, and is certainly using Zeno's formal method. From Gorgias Plato may well have borrowed.

III. MOTION

MOTION

§ A. *Place and motion*

17. Diogenes, IX. 72; Diels, fr. 4

Ζήνων δὲ τὴν κίνησιν ἀναιρεῖ λέγων τὸ κινούμενον οὔτ' ἐν ᾧ
ἐστι τόπῳ κινεῖται οὔτ' ἐν ᾧ μὴ ἔστι.

18. Epiphanius, *adv. Haer.* III. 11; Diels, *Dox.* 590. 20

καὶ λέγει ⟨sc. ὁ Ζήνων⟩ οὕτως· τὸ κινούμενον ἤτοι ἐν ᾧ ἐστι
τόπῳ κινεῖται ἢ ἐν ᾧ οὐκ ἔστι. καὶ οὔτε ἐν ᾧ ἐστι τόπῳ κινεῖται
5 οὔτε ἐν ᾧ οὐκ ἔστιν· οὐκ ἄρα τι κινεῖται.

§ B. *The four arguments on motion*

I. THE DICHOTOMY

19. Aristotle, *Phys.* Z 9. 239*b* 14; Diels, A 25

τέτταρες δ' εἰσὶ λόγοι περὶ κινήσεως Ζήνωνος οἱ παρέχοντες
τὰς δυσκολίας τοῖς λύουσι—πρῶτος μὲν ὁ περὶ τοῦ μὴ κινεῖσθαι
διὰ τὸ πρότερον εἰς τὸ ἥμισυ δεῖν ἀφικέσθαι τὸ φερόμενον ἢ πρὸς
τὸ τέλος, περὶ οὗ διείλομεν ἐν τοῖς πρότερον λόγοις. sc. *Phys.* Z 2.
10 233*a* 21 διὸ καὶ ὁ Ζήνωνος λόγος ψεῦδος λαμβάνει τὸ μὴ ἐνδέ-
χεσθαι τὰ ἄπειρα διελθεῖν ἢ ἄψασθαι τῶν ἀπείρων καθ' ἕκαστον
ἐν πεπερασμένῳ χρόνῳ. διχῶς γὰρ λέγεται καὶ τὸ μῆκος καὶ ὁ
χρόνος ἄπειρον, καὶ ὅλως πᾶν τὸ συνεχές, ἤτοι κατὰ διαίρεσιν ἢ
τοῖς ἐσχάτοις. τῶν μὲν οὖν κατὰ ποσὸν ἀπείρων οὐκ ἐνδέχεται
15 ἄψασθαι ἐν πεπερασμένῳ χρόνῳ, τῶν δὲ κατὰ διαίρεσιν ἐνδέχεται·
καὶ γὰρ αὐτὸς ὁ χρόνος οὕτως ἄπειρος. ὥστε ἐν τῷ ἀπείρῳ καὶ
οὐκ ἐν τῷ πεπερασμένῳ συμβαίνει διιέναι τὸ ἄπειρον καὶ ἅπτεσθαι
τῶν ἀπείρων τοῖς ἀπείροις, οὐ τοῖς πεπερασμένοις.

MOTION

§ A. *Place and motion*

17. Diogenes, IX. 72; Diels, fr. 4

Zeno does away with motion, saying that "what moves does not move either in the place in which it is or in the place in which it is not".

18. Epiphanius, *adv. Haer.* III. 11; Diels, *Dox.* 590. 20

Zeno argues as follows: what moves, moves either in the place in which it is, or in the place in which it is not; and it does not move 5 either in the place in which it is or in the place in which it is not; nothing therefore moves.

§ B. *The four arguments on motion*

I. THE DICHOTOMY

19. Aristotle, *Phys.* Z 9. 239*b* 14; Diels, A 25

There are four arguments of Zeno about motion which give trouble to those who try to solve the problems they involve. The first says that motion is impossible, because an object in motion 10 must reach the half-way point before it gets to the end. This we have discussed above. sc. *Phys. Z.* 2. 233*a* 21 Hence Zeno's argument makes a false assumption when it asserts that it is impossible to traverse an infinite number of positions or to make an infinite number of contacts one by one in a finite time. For there are two senses in 15 which length and time and, generally, any continuum are called infinite, namely either in respect of divisibility or of extension. So while it is impossible to make an infinite number of contacts in a finite time where the infinite is a quantitative infinite, yet it is possible where the infinite is an infinite in respect of division; for the time 20 itself is also infinite in this respect. And so we find that it is possible to traverse an infinite number of positions in a time in this sense infinite, not finite; and to make an infinite number of contacts because its moments are in this sense infinite, not finite.

44 MOTION

20. Simplicius, 1013. 4, *ad* 239*b* 10

ὁ πρῶτος ⟨sc. λόγος⟩ τοιοῦτός ἐστιν· εἰ ἔστι κίνησις ἀνάγκη
τὸ κινούμενον ἐν πεπερασμένῳ ἄπειρα διεξιέναι· τοῦτο δὲ ἀδύ-
νατον· οὐκ ἄρα ἔστιν κίνησις. ἐδείκνυ δὲ τὸ συνημμένον ἐκ τοῦ
τὸ κινούμενον διάστημά τι κινεῖσθαι· παντὸς δὲ διαστήματος ἐπ᾽
5 ἄπειρον ὄντος διαιρετοῦ τὸ κινούμενον ἀνάγκη τὸ ἥμισυ πρῶτον
διελθεῖν οὗ κινεῖται διαστήματος καὶ τότε τὸ ὅλον· ἀλλὰ καὶ πρὸ
τοῦ ἡμίσεος ὅλου τὸ ἐκείνου ἥμισυ, καὶ τούτου πάλιν τὸ ἥμισυ·
εἰ οὖν ἄπειρα τὰ ἡμίση διὰ τὸ πάντος τοῦ ληφθέντος δυνατὸν
εἶναι τὸ ἥμισυ λαβεῖν, τὰ δὲ ἄπειρα ἀδύνατον ἐν πεπερασμένῳ
10 διελθεῖν χρόνῳ· τοῦτο δὲ ὡς ἐναργὲς ἐλάμβανεν ὁ Ζήνων (τούτου
δὲ τοῦ λόγου πρότερον ἀπεμνημόνευσεν ὁ Ἀριστοτέλης λέγων
ἀδύνατον εἶναι ἐν πεπερασμένῳ τὰ ἄπειρα διελθεῖν καὶ τῶν
ἀπείρων ἅψασθαι)· ἀλλὰ μὴν πᾶν μέγεθος ἀπείρους διαιρέσεις
ἔχει· ἀδύνατον ἄρα ἐν πεπερασμένῳ χρόνῳ μέγεθός τι διελθεῖν.
15 Simplicius, 947. 5, *ad* 233 a 21 ἔστι δὲ ὁ λόγος ὁ τοῦ Ζήνωνος
τοιοῦτος· εἰ ἔστι κίνησις, ἐνδέχεται ἐν πεπερασμένῳ χρόνῳ τὰ
ἄπειρα διελθεῖν ἁπτόμενον αὐτῶν ἑκάστου· ἀλλὰ μὴν τοῦτο
ἀδύνατον· οὐκ ἄρα ἔστι κίνησις. καὶ τὸ μὲν συνημμένον ἐδείκνυ
χρώμενος τῇ τῶν μεγεθῶν ἐπ᾽ ἄπειρον διαιρέσει· εἰ γὰρ πᾶν
20 μέγεθος εἰς ἄπειρα διαιρετόν, εἴη ἂν καὶ ἐξ ἀπείρων συγκείμενον,
ὥστε τὸ κινούμενον καὶ διιὸν ὁτιοῦν μέγεθος, ἄπειρον ἂν κινοῖτο
καὶ διεξίοι καὶ ἀπείρων ἅπτοιτο ἐν πεπερασμένῳ χρόνῳ, ἐν ᾧ τὸ
ὅλον τὸ πεπερασμένον δίεισιν. "ἅψασθαι" δὲ "τῶν ἀπείρων
καθ᾽ ἕκαστον" φησίν, ἐπεὶ δύναταί τι τὰ ἄπειρα δοκεῖν διεληλυ-
25 θέναι τῷ ὑπερβαίνειν αὐτά. καὶ οὕτω μὲν τὸ συνημμένον ἐδείκνυ·
τὴν δὲ πρόσληψιν τὴν λέγουσαν ἀλλὰ μὴν ἀδύνατον τὰ ἄπειρα
διελθεῖν καὶ ἅψασθαι ἐν πεπερασμένῳ χρόνῳ δείκνυσιν ἐκ τοῦ τὸ
ἄπειρον ἀδιεξίτητον εἶναι καὶ ἐκ τοῦ μὴ δυνατὸν εἶναι ἐν πεπερασμένῳ χρόνῳ τῶν ἀπείρων ἅψασθαι, εἴ γε ἐν ἄλλῳ καὶ ἄλλῳ τοῦ
30 χρόνου ἅπτεται τὸ κινούμενον τῶν τοῦ ὑποκειμένου μερῶν.
ἀδύνατον δὲ ἑκάστου ἅψασθαι τῶν ἀπείρων εἶπεν διότι ὁ ἁπτόμενος
οἷον ἀριθμεῖ· ἀριθμῆσαι δὲ ἀδύνατον τὰ ἄπειρα.

20. Simplicius, 1013. 4, *ad* 239*b* 10

The first argument is the following: If there is motion, then a moving object must in a finite time complete an infinite number of positions, but since this is impossible there is no motion. He proves his hypothesis thus: An object in motion must move through a certain distance; but since every distance is infinitely divisible the 5 moving object must first traverse half the distance through which it is moving, and then the whole distance; but before it traverses the whole of the half distance, it must traverse half of the half, and again half of this half. If then these halves are infinite in number, because it is always possible to halve any given length, and if it is impossible 10 to traverse an infinite number of positions in a finite time—this Zeno assumed as self-evident; and Aristotle has previously referred to his argument when he speaks of it being impossible to traverse an infinite number of positions or to make an infinite number of contacts in a finite time—anyhow, to resume, every magnitude has 15 an infinite number of subdivisions, and therefore it is impossible to traverse any magnitude in a finite time.

Simplicius, 947. 5, *ad* 233*a* 21 Zeno's argument is the following: If there is motion, it is possible in a finite time to traverse an infinite number of positions, making an infinite number of contacts one by 20 one; but this is impossible, and therefore there is no motion. His hypothesis he proved by means of the infinite divisibility of magnitude. For if every magnitude is infinitely divisible, it will be made up of an infinite number of parts, and so a body, moving through and traversing a distance of given magnitude, will move through and 25 complete an infinite number of positions and make an infinite number of contacts in a finite time, that is, in the time it takes to move through the whole finite distance. He says "to make an infinite number of contacts one by one", because it might seem that a body traversed an infinite number of positions by passing *over* them without 30 making *contact* with each. In this way he proves the hypothesis. The minor premiss, which says "but it is impossible (1) to traverse an infinite number of positions or (2) to make an infinite number of contacts in a finite time", he proves (1) from the interminability of the infinite and (2) from the impossibility of making an infinite 35 number of contacts in a finite time, if the moving object makes contact with the successive parts of the distance in question at successive moments of time; for he said that it is impossible to make contact with each member of an infinite collection because the person making the contacts is as it were counting, and it is impossible to 40 count infinite collections.

21. Philoponus, 802. 31, *ad* 233 *a* 21

ὁ Ζήνων ἀναιρῶν τὸ εἶναι κίνησιν ἐκέχρητο τοιούτῳ συλλογισμῷ· εἰ ἔστι κίνησις, ἐνδέχεται τὸ ἄπειρον ἐν πεπερασμένῳ χρόνῳ διελθεῖν, ἀλλὰ μὴν τοῦτο ἀδύνατον, οὐκ ἄρα ἔστι κίνησις. εἰ γὰρ κινοῖτό τι ἐπὶ πηχυαίου μεγέθους ἐν μίᾳ ὥρᾳ, ἐπειδὴ ἐν
5 παντὶ μεγέθει ἄπειρά ἐστι σημεῖα, ἀνάγκη ἄρα πάντων ἅψασθαι τῶν σημείων τοῦ μεγέθους τὸ κινούμενον· διελεύσεται ἄρα τὰ ἄπειρα ἐν πεπερασμένῳ χρόνῳ, ὅπερ ἀδύνατον.

Philoponus, 81. 7, *ad* 187 *a* 1 ὅτι δὲ τὸ ἓν τοῦτο καὶ ἀκίνητόν ἐστιν, ἐκέχρητο λόγῳ τοιούτῳ. εἰ κινεῖταί τι, φησί, τήνδε τὴν πεπερασμέ-
10 νην γραμμήν, ἀνάγκη πᾶσα πρὶν τὴν ὅλην κινηθῆναι, τὴν ἡμίσειαν κινηθῆναι, καὶ πρὶν τὸ ἥμισυ τῆς ὅλης κινηθῆναι, ἀνάγκη πρότερον τὸ τέταρτον, καὶ πρὸ τοῦ τετάρτου τὸ ὄγδοον, καὶ τοῦτο ἐπ' ἄπειρον· τὸ γὰρ συνεχὲς ἐπ' ἄπειρόν ἐστι διαιρετόν. ἀνάγκη ἄρα εἰ κινεῖταί τι πεπερασμένην γραμμήν, ἄπειρά τινα κινηθῆναι μεγέθη πρό-
15 τερον· εἰ δὲ τοῦτο, πᾶσα δὲ κίνησις ἔν τινι χρόνῳ πεπερασμένῳ γίνεται (οὐδὲν γὰρ ἐν τῷ ἀπείρῳ χρόνῳ κινεῖται), ἔσται ἄρα τὰ ἄπειρα μεγέθη κινηθῆναι ἐν πεπερασμένῳ χρόνῳ, ὅπερ ἀδύνατον· ὅλως δὲ τὸ ἄπειρον ἀδιεξίτητον.

22. Themistius, 186. 30, *ad* 233 *a* 21

τοῦτο δὲ ἀγνοεῖ Ζήνων ἢ προσποιεῖται, ὅταν οἴηται τὴν κίνησιν
20 ἀναιρεῖν ἐκ τοῦ μὴ δυνατὸν εἶναι λέγειν ἐν πεπερασμένῳ τῷ χρόνῳ τὰ ἄπειρα διελθεῖν τὸ κινούμενον καὶ ἅψασθαι τὸ Α ἀπείρων καὶ καθ' ἕκαστον, εἰ τὸ μὲν μῆκος τὸ ποδιαῖον εἰς ἄπειρα διαιρετὸν καὶ ἐπ' ἄπειρον, ὁ δὲ χρόνος τῆς κινήσεως τῆς ἐπ' αὐτῷ πεπερασμένος.

23. Aristotle, *Phys.* Θ 8. 263 *a* 5
25 τὸν αὐτὸν δὲ τρόπον ἀπαντητέον καὶ πρὸς τοὺς ἐρωτῶντας τὸν Ζήνωνος λόγον, καὶ ἀξιοῦντας, εἰ ἀεὶ τὸ ἥμισυ διιέναι δεῖ, ταῦτα

21. Philoponus, 802. 31, *ad* 233*a* 21

Zeno in doing away with the reality of motion made use of the following syllogism. If there is motion, it is possible to traverse an infinity of positions in a finite time; but this is impossible; therefore there is no motion. For suppose a thing moves over the length of a cubit in one hour: then, since there are an infinite number of points 5 in every magnitude, the moving object must make contact with all these points in the course of its movement: it will therefore traverse an infinite number of positions in a finite time, which is impossible.

Philoponus, 81. 7, *ad* 187*a* 1 To show that this one is also un-moved, he made use of the following argument. If anything moves 10 along a given finite straight line, it must, before moving along the whole of it, move along the half of it, and, before moving along the half of the whole, it must first move along a quarter of it, and before a quarter an eighth, and so on *ad infinitum*; for the continuum is infinitely divisible. So if anything moves along a finite straight line, 15 it must, before completing its movement, have moved through an infinite number of magnitudes: but if this is so, and if every move-ment occupies a definite finite time (for there is no motion that occupies an infinite time), then we find that in a finite time a motion through an infinite number of magnitudes has taken place, 20 which is an impossibility; for the infinite is interminable absolutely.

22. Themistius, 186. 30, *ad* 233*a* 21

Of this Zeno either is or pretends to be ignorant, when he sup-poses he does away with motion by saying that it is impossible for a moving body to traverse an infinite number of positions in a finite time and for a body *A* to make an infinite number of contacts 25 one by one; for the foot length is divisible into an infinite number of parts and *ad infinitum*, but the time taken by a motion through this distance is finite.

23. Aristotle, *Phys.* Θ 8. 263*a* 5

The same method should be adopted in replying to those who put Zeno's puzzle, and claim that in traversing any distance we must 30

δ' ἄπειρα, τὰ δ' ἄπειρα ἀδύνατον διεξελθεῖν, ἢ ὡς τὸν αὐτὸν
τοῦτον λόγον τινὲς ἄλλως ἐρωτῶσι, ἀξιοῦντες ἅμα τῷ κινεῖσθαι
τὴν ἡμίσειαν πρότερον ἀριθμεῖν καθ' ἕκαστον γιγνόμενον τὸ
ἥμισυ, ὥστε διελθόντος τὴν ὅλην ἄπειρον συμβαίνει ἠριθμηκέναι
5 ἀριθμόν· τοῦτο δ' ὁμολογουμένως ἐστὶν ἀδύνατον.

24. Simplicius, 1289. 5, ad 263 a 5

ἦν δὲ ὁ μὲν ὑπὸ Ζήνωνος λεγόμενος λόγος, οὗ νῦν μνημονεύει,
τοιοῦτος· 'εἰ ἔστι κίνησις, ἔσται τι τὸ ἐν πεπερασμένῳ χρόνῳ
ἄπειρα διεληλυθός· τῷ γὰρ ἐπ' ἄπειρον εἶναι τὴν διχοτομίαν ἐν
παντὶ συνεχεῖ ἔσται ἄπειρα ἡμίση τῷ πᾶν μόριον αὐτοῦ ἥμισυ
10 ἔχειν. ἔσται δὴ τὸ κεκινημένον τὴν πεπερασμένην τὰ ἄπειρα
ἡμίση διεληλυθὸς ἐν πεπερασμένῳ χρόνῳ, ἐν ᾧ διῆλθε τὴν
πεπερασμένην. προσλαμβάνων δὲ τὸ ἀντικείμενον τοῦ ἐν τῷ
συνημμένῳ ἑπομένου τὸ μὴ δύνασθαί τι ἐν πεπερασμένῳ χρόνῳ
ἄπειρά τινα διεξελθεῖν, διότι οὐδὲ διεξελθεῖν ὅλως οἷόν τε τὰ
15 ἄπειρα, ἀνήρει τὸ εἶναι κίνησιν.' οὕτω μὲν οὖν ὁ Ζήνων. τινὰς
δὲ ἄλλως ἐρωτᾶν αὐτόν φησι λέγοντας· 'εἰ ἔστι κίνησις, ἐπεὶ
ἔστιν ἄπειρα ἡμίση ἐν παντὶ συνεχεῖ, τὸ κινούμενον ἐπὶ τοῦ
συνεχοῦς δυνατὸν καθ' ἕκαστον ἥμισυ ἀριθμεῖν. τούτου δὲ γινο-
μένου, ὅταν τὸ κινούμενον διεληλυθὸς ᾖ τὸ πεπερασμένον μέγεθος,
20 ἔσται ὁ ἀριθμῶν ἄπειρα ἡμίση ἠριθμηκώς. εἰ οὖν τοῦτο ἀδύνατον
τὸ ἀριθμῆσαι τὰ ἄπειρα, ἀδύνατον ἂν εἴη καὶ τὸ ᾧ τοῦτο ἔπεται,
εἵπετο δὲ τῷ κίνησιν εἶναι.'

25. [Aristotle], *De Lin. Insec.* 968 a 18

One of the arguments used by the supporters of the ἄτομοι
γραμμαί. ἔτι δὲ κατὰ τὸν Ζήνωνος λόγον ἀνάγκη τι μέγεθος
25 ἀμερὲς εἶναι, εἵπερ ἀδύνατον μὲν ἐν πεπερασμένῳ χρόνῳ ἀπείρων
ἅψασθαι, καθ' ἕκαστον ἁπτόμενον, ἀνάγκη δ' ἐπὶ τὸ ἥμισυ πρότερον ἀφικνεῖσθαι τὸ κινούμενον, τοῦ δὲ μὴ ἀμεροῦς πάντως
ἔστιν ἥμισυ.

first traverse the half of it, that these subdivisions are infinite, and
that it is impossible to complete an infinite number of distances: or,
as some, who put the puzzle in a different form, claim, that in the
course of its motion the moving body must, as it reaches each
half-way point, count the half of this half, so that when it has moved 5
through the whole distance it has counted an infinite number—
which is admittedly impossible.

24. Simplicius, 1289. 5, *ad* 263 *a* 5

The argument of Zeno, to which he now refers, was as follows:
If there is motion there will be something which has traversed an
infinite number of positions in a finite time; for, since the process 10
of dichotomy can continue infinitely, in every continuum there will
be an infinite number of halves owing to every part of it having a
half. A body therefore which has moved over a finite distance will
have traversed an infinite number of halves in a finite time, that is,
in the time which it took to traverse the finite distance in question. 15
He then goes on to assume the opposite of the consequence that
follows from his hypothesis, i.e. he assumes that it is impossible to
get to the end of an infinite number of positions in a finite time,
because it is impossible absolutely to exhaust any infinite collection,
and so does away with the reality of motion. So Zeno argued: but 20
some, Aristotle says, put the puzzle in a different way, as follows:
'If there is motion, since there is an infinite number of halves in any
continuum, a body moving through a continuum should be able to
count each of these halves as it comes to it. But if this is so, then
when the moving body has traversed the finite magnitude in ques- 25
tion, the counter will have counted an infinite number of halves. If
therefore it is impossible to count an infinite number, then any
premiss from which this follows as conclusion must be impossible;
but the premiss from which it followed was the supposition that
motion is real.'   30

25. [Aristotle], *De Lin. Insec.* 968 *a* 18

Further they suppose that the necessary result of Zeno's argument
is that there must be some indivisible magnitude. For it is impossible
to make an infinite number of contacts one by one in a finite time:
but a moving body must first reach the half-way point of any distance, and there is always a half of any distance not absolutely 35
indivisible.

II. The Achilles

26. Aristotle, *Phys.* Z 9. 239*b* 14; Diels, A 26

δεύτερος δὲ ὁ καλούμενος ᾿Αχιλλεύς. ἔστι δ᾿ οὗτος ὅτι τὸ βραδύτατον[1] οὐδέποτε καταληφθήσεται θέον ὑπὸ τοῦ ταχίστου· ἔμπροσθεν γὰρ ἀναγκαῖον ἐλθεῖν τὸ διῶκον ὅθεν ὥρμησε τὸ φεῦγον, ὥστ᾿ ἀεί τι προέχειν ἀναγκαῖον τὸ βραδύτατον. ἔστι δὲ 5 καὶ οὗτος ὁ αὐτὸς τῷ διχοτομεῖν, διαφέρει δὲ ἐν τῷ διαιρεῖν μὴ δίχα τὸ προσλαμβανόμενον μέγεθος. τὸ μὲν οὖν μὴ καταλαμβάνεσθαι τὸ βραδύτερον συμβέβηκεν ἐκ τοῦ λόγου, γίγνεται δὲ παρὰ ταὐτὸ τῇ διχοτομίᾳ—ἐν ἀμφοτέροις γὰρ συμβαίνει μὴ ἀφικνεῖσθαι πρὸς τὸ πέρας διαιρουμένου πως τοῦ μεγέθους· ἀλλὰ 10 πρόσκειται ἐν τούτῳ ὅτι οὐδὲ τὸ τάχιστον τετραγῳδημένον ἐν τῷ διώκειν τὸ βραδύτατον—ὥστ᾿ ἀνάγκη καὶ τὴν λύσιν εἶναι τὴν αὐτήν.

27. Simplicius, 1013. 31, *ad loc.*

καὶ οὗτος ὁ λόγος ἐκ τῆς ἐπ᾿ ἄπειρον διαιρέσεως ἐπικεχείρηται κατ᾿ ἄλλην διασκευήν. καὶ εἴη ἂν τοιοῦτος· εἰ ἔστι κίνησις, τὸ 15 βραδύτατον ὑπὸ τοῦ ταχίστου οὐδέποτε καταληφθήσεται· ἀλλὰ μὴν τοῦτο ἀδύνατον· οὐκ ἄρα ἔστι κίνησις.... (1014. 9) ᾿Αχιλλεὺς οὖν ὁ λόγος ἀπὸ τοῦ παραληφθέντος ἐν αὐτῷ ᾿Αχιλλέως ἐκλήθη, ὃν ἀδύνατόν φησιν ὁ λόγος τὴν χελώνην διώκοντα καταλαβεῖν. καὶ γὰρ ἀνάγκη μὲν τὸ καταληψόμενον πρὸ τοῦ καταλαβεῖν εἰς 20 τὸ πέρας ἐλθεῖν πρῶτον, ὅθεν ἐξώρμησε τὸ φεῦγον. ἐν ᾧ δὲ τὸ διῶκον ἐπὶ τοῦτο παραγίνεται, ἐν τούτῳ τὸ φεῦγον πρόεισί τι διάστημα, εἰ καὶ ἔλαττον οὗ προῆλθεν τὸ διῶκον τῷ βραδύτερον εἶναι· ἀλλ᾿ οὖν πρόεισιν· οὐ γὰρ ἠρεμεῖ. καὶ ἐν ᾧ πάλιν χρόνῳ τοῦτο δίεισι τὸ διῶκον ὃ προῆλθε τὸ φεῦγον, ἐν τούτῳ πάλιν τῷ 25 χρόνῳ δίεισί τι τὸ φεῦγον τοσούτῳ ἔλαττον οὗ πρότερον ἐκινήθη, ὅσῳ βραδύτερόν ἐστιν αὐτὸ τοῦ διώκοντος. καὶ οὕτως ἐν παντὶ χρόνῳ ἐν ᾧ τὸ διῶκον δίεισιν, ὃ προελήλυθε τὸ φεῦγον βραδύτερον ὄν, ἐν τούτῳ πρόεισί τι καὶ τὸ φεῦγον· κἂν γὰρ ἀεὶ ἔλαττον, ἀλλ᾿ οὖν δίεισί τι καὶ αὐτὸ κινούμενον ὅλως. τῷ δὲ ἐπ᾿ ἄπειρον 30 ἔλαττον ἄλλο ἄλλου διάστημα λαμβάνειν διὰ τὴν ἐπ᾿ ἄπειρον τῶν μεγεθῶν τομήν, οὐ μόνον Ἕκτωρ ὑπὸ τοῦ ᾿Αχιλλέως οὐ καταληφθήσεται, ἀλλ᾿ οὐδὲ ἡ χελώνη.

[1] Following the Loeb note *ad loc.* I have emended the βραδύτερον of Bekker's text to βραδύτατον, both here and in l. 4 (at l. 11 Bekker reads βραδύτατον).

II. THE ACHILLES

26. Aristotle, *Phys.* Z 9. 239*b* 14; Diels, A 26.

The second is the so-called Achilles. This is that the slowest runner will never be overtaken by the swiftest, since the pursuer must first reach the point from which the pursued started, and so the slower must always be ahead. This argument is essentially the same as that depending on dichotomy, but differs in that the successively 5 given lengths are not divided into halves. The conclusion of the argument is that the slowest runner is not overtaken, but it proceeds on the same lines as the dichotomy argument (for in both, by dividing the distance in a given way, we conclude that the goal is not reached: only in the Achilles a dramatic effect is produced by saying that not 10 even the swiftest will be successful in its pursuit of the slowest) and so the solution of it must be the same.

27. Simplicius, 1013. 31, *ad loc.*

This argument also bases its attempted proof on infinite divisibility but is arranged differently. It runs as follows: If there is movement the slowest will never be overtaken by the swiftest: 15 but this is impossible: therefore there is no motion....(1014. 9) The argument is called the Achilles because of the introduction into it of Achilles, who, the argument says, cannot possibly overtake the tortoise he is pursuing. For the overtaker must, before he overtakes the pursued, first come to the point from which the 20 pursued started. But during the time taken by the pursuer to reach this point, the pursued advances a certain distance; even if this distance is less than that covered by the pursuer, because the pursued is the slower of the two, yet none the less it does advance, for it is not at rest. And again during the time which the pursuer takes to 25 cover this distance which the pursued has advanced, the pursued again covers a certain distance which is proportionately smaller than the last, according as its speed is slower than that of the pursuer. And so, during every period of time in which the pursuer is covering the distance which the pursued moving at its lower relative speed 30 has already advanced, the pursued advances a yet further distance; for even though this distance decreases at each step, yet, since the pursued is also definitely in motion, it does advance some positive distance. And so by taking distances decreasing in a given proportion *ad infinitum* because of the infinite divisibility of magnitudes, we arrive at the conclusion that not only will Hector never be over- 35 taken by Achilles, but not even the tortoise.

III. THE ARROW

28. Aristotle, *Phys.* Z 9. 239*b* 30

τρίτος δ' ὁ νῦν ῥηθείς, ὅτι ἡ ὀιστὸς φερομένη ἕστηκεν. συμβαίνει δὲ παρὰ τὸ λαμβάνειν τὸν χρόνον συγκεῖσθαι ἐκ τῶν νῦν· μὴ διδομένου γὰρ τούτου οὐκ ἔσται ὁ συλλογισμός.

29. Aristotle, *Phys.* Z 9. 239*b* 5

Ζήνων δὲ παραλογίζεται· εἰ γὰρ ἀεί, φησίν, ἠρεμεῖ πᾶν ἢ
5 κινεῖται¹ ⟨οὐδὲν δὲ κινεῖται⟩² ὅταν ᾖ κατὰ τὸ ἴσον, ἔστι δ' ἀεὶ τὸ
φερόμενον ἐν τῷ νῦν κατὰ τὸ ἴσον,³ ἀκίνητον τὴν φερομένην
ὀιστόν. τοῦτο δ' ἔσται ψεῦδος· οὐ γὰρ συγκεῖται ὁ χρόνος ἐκ τῶν
νῦν τῶν ἀδιαιρέτων, ὥσπερ οὐδ' ἄλλο μέγεθος οὐδέν.

30. Simplicius, 1015. 19, *ad* 239*b* 30

τὸ φερόμενον βέλος ἐν τῷ φέρεσθαι ἵσταται, εἵπερ ἀνάγκη πᾶν
10 ἢ κινεῖσθαι ἢ ἠρεμεῖν, τὸ δὲ φερόμενον ἀεὶ κατὰ τὸ ἴσον ἑαυτῷ
ἐστι. τὸ δὲ ἀεὶ κατὰ τὸ ἴσον ἑαυτῷ ὂν οὐ κινεῖται· ἠρεμεῖ ἄρα.

31. Simplicius, 1011. 19, *ad* 239*b* 5

ὁ δὲ Ζήνωνος λόγος προλαβών, ὅτι πᾶν ὅταν ᾖ κατὰ τὸ ἴσον
ἑαυτῷ ἢ κινεῖται ἢ ἠρεμεῖ, καὶ ὅτι οὐδὲν ἐν τῷ νῦν κινεῖται, καὶ
ὅτι τὸ φερόμενον ἀεὶ ἐν τῷ ἴσῳ αὑτῷ ἐστι καθ' ἕκαστον νῦν,
15 ἐῴκει συλλογίζεσθαι οὕτως· τὸ φερόμενον βέλος ἐν παντὶ νῦν
κατὰ τὸ ἴσον ἑαυτῷ ἔστιν, ὥστε καὶ ἐν παντὶ τῷ χρόνῳ· τὸ δὲ
ἐν τῷ νῦν κατὰ τὸ ἴσον ἑαυτῷ ὂν οὐ κινεῖται, ἐπειδὴ μηδὲν ἐν
τῷ νῦν κινεῖται· τὸ δὲ μὴ κινούμενον ἠρεμεῖ, ἐπειδὴ πᾶν ἢ
κινεῖται ἢ ἠρεμεῖ· τὸ ἄρα φερόμενον βέλος, ἕως φέρεται, ἠρεμεῖ
20 κατὰ πάντα τὸν τῆς φορᾶς χρόνον.

---

¹ ἢ κινεῖται. In all the manuscripts, as in Simplicius and Philoponus (below, Nos. 31, 32). Zeller, on the ground that Zeno's premiss is a definition of rest, ejected the words. Themistius omits them (below, No. 34).
² ⟨οὐδὲν δὲ κινεῖται⟩ Diels.

III. The Arrow

28. Aristotle, *Phys.* Z 9. 239*b* 30

The third is that just given above, that the flying arrow is at rest. This conclusion follows from the assumption that time is composed of instants; for if this is not granted the conclusion cannot be inferred.

29. Aristotle, *Phys.* Z 9. 239*b* 5

Zeno's argument is fallacious. For if, he says, everything is either 5 at rest or in motion, but nothing is in motion when it occupies a space equal to itself, and what is in flight is always at any given instant occupying a space equal to itself, then the flying arrow is motionless. But this is false, for time is not composed of indivisible instants any more than any other magnitude is composed of in- 10 divisibles.

30. Simplicius, 1015. 19, *ad* 239*b* 30

The flying missile is at rest during its flight, if everything must either be in motion or at rest, but an object in flight always occupies a space equal to itself. But what always occupies a space equal to itself is not in motion, it is therefore at rest. 15

31. Simplicius, 1011. 19, *ad* 239*b* 5

Zeno's argument after making the preliminary assumptions that everything when it occupies a space equal to itself is either in motion or at rest, that nothing is in motion in the instant, and that an object in flight occupies at each instant a space equal to itself, seems to infer as follows: The flying missile occupies a space equal to itself 20 at each instant, and so during the whole time of its flight: what occupies a space equal to itself at an instant is not in motion, since nothing is in motion at an instant: but what is not in motion is at rest, since everything is either in motion or at rest: therefore the flying missile, while it is in flight, is at rest during the whole time of its flight. 25

---

3 ἐν τῷ νῦν τῷ κατὰ τὸ ἴσον rcF: τῷ κατὰ τὸ ἴσον om. cett. Bekker.
Diels (*Vors.* 19. A. 27) has the following readings: ἢ κινεῖται ⟨οὐδὲν δὲ κινεῖται⟩ ὅταν ἦ κατὰ τὸ ἴσον, ἔστι δ᾽ ἀεὶ τὸ φερόμενον ἐν τῷ νῦν, ⟨πᾶν δὲ κατὰ τὸ ἴσον ἐν τῷ νῦν⟩, κ.τ.λ. (cf. Philop. 817. 6, *ad* 239*b* 6 εἶτα πρόσθες πᾶν δὲ τὸ ἐν τῷ νῦν ἐν τῷ ἴσῳ ἑαυτοῦ ὑπάρχει τόπῳ).

32. Simplicius, 1034. 4

ἐκ δὲ τούτου καὶ τὸν Ζήνωνος ἔλυσε λόγον τὸν λέγοντα εἰ τὸ
φερόμενον βέλος ἀεὶ κατὰ τὸ ἴσον ἑαυτῷ ἐστί, τὸ δὲ κατὰ τὸ
ἴσον ἑαυτῷ χρόνον τινὰ ὂν ἠρεμεῖ, τὸ φερόμενον βέλος ἕως ἂν
κινῆται ἠρεμεῖ.

33. Philoponus, 816. 30, ad 239b 5

5 ἅπαν, φησίν, ἐν τῷ ἴσῳ ἑαυτοῦ τόπῳ ὑπάρχον ἢ ἠρεμεῖ ἢ
κινεῖται, ἀδύνατον δὲ ἐν τῷ ἴσῳ ἑαυτοῦ κινεῖσθαι, ἠρεμεῖ ἄρα. τὸ
τοίνυν φερόμενον βέλος ἐν ἑκάστῳ τῶν νῦν τοῦ χρόνου καθ' ὃν
κινεῖται ἐν ἴσῳ ἑαυτοῦ τόπῳ ὑπάρχον ἠρεμήσει, εἰ δὲ ἐν πᾶσι
τοῖς τοῦ χρόνου νῦν ἀπείροις οὖσιν ἠρεμεῖ, καὶ ἐν παντὶ ἠρε-
10 μήσει. ἀλλ' ὑπόκειται κινούμενον· τὸ βέλος ἄρα κινούμενον
ἠρεμήσει.

34. Themistius, 199. 4, ad 239b 1

εἰ γὰρ ἠρεμεῖ, φησίν, ἅπαντα, ὅταν ᾖ κατὰ τὸ ἴσον αὑτῷ
διάστημα ἔστι δὲ ἀεὶ τὸ φερόμενον κατὰ τὸ ἴσον ἑαυτῷ διάστημα,
ἀκίνητον ἀνάγκη τὴν οἰστὸν εἶναι τὴν φερομένην.

Themistius, 200. 29, adds nothing.

IV. The Stadium

35. Aristotle, Phys. Z 9. 239b 33

15 τέταρτος δ' ὁ περὶ τῶν ἐν σταδίῳ κινουμένων ἐξ ἐναντίας
ἴσων ὄγκων παρ' ἴσους, τῶν μὲν ἀπὸ τέλους τοῦ σταδίου τῶν δ'
ἀπὸ μέσου, ἴσῳ τάχει, ἐν ᾧ συμβαίνειν οἴεται ἴσον εἶναι χρόνον
τῷ διπλασίῳ τὸν ἥμισυν. ἔστι δ' ὁ παραλογισμὸς ἐν τῷ τὸ μὲν
παρὰ κινούμενον τὸ δὲ παρ' ἠρεμοῦν τὸ ἴσον μέγεθος ἀξιοῦν τῷ
20 ἴσῳ τάχει τὸν ἴσον φέρεσθαι χρόνον · τοῦτο δ' ἐστὶ ψεῦδος. οἷον
ἔστωσαν οἱ ἑστῶτες ἴσοι ὄγκοι ἐφ' ὧν τὰ ΑΑ, οἱ δ' ἐφ' ὧν τὰ
ΒΒ ἀρχόμενοι ἀπὸ τοῦ μέσου [τῶν Α¹], ἴσοι τὸν ἀριθμὸν τούτοις

1 Om. EHI, Ross. τῶν A cett: cf. Simp. 1017. 4.

32. Simplicius, 1034. 4

By this reasoning also he disproved Zeno's argument that if the
flying missile always occupies a space equal to itself, and if what
occupies for any time a space equal to itself is at rest, then the flying
missile is at rest all the time it is in motion.

33. Philoponus, 816. 30, *ad* 239*b* 5

Everything, he says, that occupies a space equal to itself is either 5
at rest or in motion; but it is impossible for anything to be in motion
when it occupies a space equal to itself, and it is therefore at rest.
The flying missile, therefore, at every instant of the time during
which it is in motion occupies a space equal to itself and so is at rest;
but if it is at rest at all the instants of this time, which are infinite 10
in number, it will be at rest during the whole time. But it was
supposed to be in motion: and our conclusion is therefore that the
moving missile is at rest.

34. Themistius, 199. 4, *ad* 239*b* 1

For if, he says, everything is at rest, when it occupies an extension
equal to itself, but an object in flight always occupies an extension 15
equal to itself, then the flying arrow must be motionless.

IV. The Stadium

35. Aristotle, *Phys.* Z 9. 239 *b* 33

The fourth is the one about the two rows of equal bodies which
move past each other in a stadium with equal velocities in opposite
directions, the one row originally stretching from the goal ⟨to the
middle-point⟩ of the stadium, the other from the middle-point ⟨to 20
the starting post⟩. This, he thinks, involves the conclusion that half
a given time is equal to its double ⟨i.e. the whole time⟩. The fallacy
lies in assuming that a body takes an equal time to pass with equal
velocity a body that is in motion and a body of equal size at rest,
an assumption which is false. For example, let *AA* be the stationary 25
bodies of equal size, let *BB* be the bodies, equal in number and size

ὄντες καὶ τὸ μέγεθος, οἱ δ' ἐφ' ὧν τὰ ΓΓ ἀπὸ τοῦ ἐσχάτου, ἴσοι
τὸν ἀριθμὸν ὄντες τούτοις καὶ τὸ μέγεθος, καὶ ἰσοταχεῖς τοῖς Β.
συμβαίνει δὴ[1] τὸ πρῶτον Β ἅμα ἐπὶ τῷ ἐσχάτῳ εἶναι καὶ τὸ
πρῶτον Γ, παρ' ἄλληλα κινουμένων. συμβαίνει δὲ[2] τὸ Γ παρὰ
5 πάντα τὰ Β[3] διεξεληλυθέναι, τὸ δὲ Β[4] παρὰ τὰ ἡμίση· ὥστε
ἥμισυν εἶναι τὸν χρόνον· ἴσον γὰρ ἑκάτερόν ἐστι παρ' ἕκαστον.
ἅμα δὲ συμβαίνει τὸ πρῶτον Β[5] παρὰ πάντα τὰ Γ παρεληλυθέναι·
ἅμα γὰρ ἔσται τὸ πρῶτον Γ καὶ τὸ πρῶτον Β ἐπὶ τοῖς ἐναντίοις
ἐσχάτοις, [ἴσον χρόνον παρ' ἕκαστον γιγνόμενον τῶν Β[6] ὅσον-
10 περ τῶν Α, ὥς φησι[7],] διὰ τὸ ἀμφότερα ἴσον χρόνον παρὰ τὰ Α[8]
γίγνεσθαι. ὁ μὲν οὖν λόγος οὗτός ἐστιν, συμβαίνει δὲ παρὰ τὸ
εἰρημένον ψεῦδος.

36. Simplicius, 1016. 9–1019. 9, *ad loc.*

καὶ ὁ τέταρτος τῶν περὶ κινήσεως τοῦ Ζήνωνος λόγων εἰς
ἀδύνατον ἀπάγων καὶ οὗτος τὸ εἶναι κίνησιν τοιοῦτός τις ἦν· εἰ
15 ἔστι κίνησις, τῶν ἴσων μεγεθῶν καὶ ἰσοταχῶν τὸ ἕτερον τοῦ
ἑτέρου ἐν τῷ αὐτῷ χρόνῳ διπλασίαν κίνησιν κινήσεται καὶ οὐκ
ἴσην. καὶ ἔστι μὲν καὶ τοῦτο ἄτοπον, ἄτοπον δὲ καὶ τὸ τούτῳ
ἑπόμενον τὸ τὸν αὐτὸν καὶ ἴσον χρόνον ἅμα διπλάσιόν τε καὶ
ἥμισυ εἶναι. δείκνυσι δὲ αὐτὸ ὁμολογούμενον λαβὼν τὸ τὰ
20 ἰσοταχῆ καὶ ἴσα ἐν τῷ ἴσῳ χρόνῳ ἴσον διάστημα κεκινῆσθαι·
καὶ ἔτι μέντοι τῶν ἰσοταχῶν τε καὶ ἴσων, ἂν τὸ μὲν ἥμισυ, τὸ
δὲ διπλάσιον ᾗ κεκινημένον, ἐν ἡμίσει μὲν χρόνῳ τὸ ἥμισυ, ἐν
διπλασίῳ δὲ τὸ διπλάσιον εἶναι κεκινημένον. τούτων προλη-

[1] δὲ FHK: Simp. 1017. 29, Alex. *apud* Simp. 1019. 27. δὴ cett.
[2] δὲ E¹FHK: Simp. 1017. 29, Alex. *apud* Simp. 1019. 27. δὴ cett.
Bekker.
[3] πάντα τὰ *A*, FKE²: Simp. 1018. 1, Alex. *apud* Simp. 1019. 28.
πάντα τὰ *B*, E¹HI Bekker.
[4] τὸ δὲ *B*, E: Simp. 1018. 1, Alex. *apud* Simp. 1019. 29. τὰ δὲ *B*,
FkHI Bekker.
[5] τὸ αβ E: τὰ *B* cett., Simp. 1019. 13, Bekker: τὸ *B* Ross. I take τὸ
πρῶτον β to be the true reading, and suppose that this was at some time

to the *A*s, stretching from the middle-point ⟨of the stadium to the starting post⟩, and *CC* those stretching from the goal ⟨to the middle-point⟩, being equal in number and size to the *A*s, and moving with a velocity equal to that of the *B*s. Then it follows that, as *B*s and *C*s move past each other, the first *B* reaches the last *C* at the same time 5 as the first *C* reaches the last *B*. And it follows that the first *C* has passed all the *B*s, the first *B* half that number of bodies ⟨viz. two *A*s⟩: and so the first *B* has taken only half the time ⟨that the first *C* has taken⟩, since each takes an equal time in passing each body. And it follows that at the same moment the first *B* has passed all the *C*s: 10 for the first *C* and the first *B* will arrive simultaneously at the opposite end *A*s, since both take an equal time passing the *A*s. This then is his argument, and it rests on the above-mentioned fallacy.

36. Simplicius, 1016. 9–1019. 9, *ad loc.*

The fourth of Zeno's arguments about motion, which also leads to the conclusion that it is impossible for motion to be a reality, was 15 as follows: If there is motion, of two bodies of equal size and moving with equal velocities, one will move twice as far as the other, and not the same distance, in the same time. This is of course an absurd conclusion, but so also is the conclusion that follows upon this that the time they take, which is equal and the same, is at once both 20 double and half. In his proof he assumes as admitted that bodies moving with an equal velocity and of equal size move an equal distance in equal times, and further that of such bodies, if one moves half as far as the other, then the motion of the first will occupy half the time of that of the second. This being premised he goes on to 25

---

written τὸ αβ (cf. Simp. 1017. 15 and crit. note 2, where certain manuscripts have τοῦ αβ instead of τοῦ πρώτου β). This accounts naturally enough for the τὰ β of the other MSS. [This reading was suggested to me by Prof. Cornford, who has incorporated it into the text of the Loeb *Physics*.]

[6] τῶν *Γ* Loeb: τῶν *B* codd.

[7] Om.ἴσον χρόνον... ὥς φησι as a gloss on ἴσον γὰρ ἑκατερόν ἐστι παρ' ἕκαστον in l. 6: Ross.

[8] κατὰ τὸ *A* Alex. *apud* Simp. 1019. 32. παρὰ τὰ *A* codd.

φθέντων στάδιον ὑπετίθετο οἷον τὸ ΔΕ, καὶ τέσσαρα μεγέθη ἢ ὁσαοῦν, ἄρτια μόνον, ὥστε ἔχειν ἥμισυ ἰσόογκα (ὡς δὲ ὁ Εὔδημός

```
        Α Α Α Α
  Δ  │  Β Β Β Β  ──→  │  Ε
     │  ←──  Γ Γ Γ Γ  │
```

φησι, κύβους) ἐφ᾽ ὧν τὰ Α, ὡς τὸ μέσον διάστημα ἐπέχειν τοῦ σταδίου ἑστῶτα ταῦτα. ὧν ἑστώτων πρῶτον ὁρίζει τὸ πρὸς τῇ 5 ἀρχῇ τοῦ σταδίου τῇ κατὰ τὸ Δ, ἔσχατον δὲ τὸ πρὸς τῷ Ε, καὶ λαμβάνει ἄλλους τέσσαρας ὄγκους ἢ κύβους ἴσους τοῖς ἑστῶσι καὶ τὸ μέγεθος καὶ τὸν ἀριθμὸν ἐφ᾽ ὧν τὰ Β, ἀρχομένους μὲν ἀπὸ ἀρχῆς τοῦ σταδίου, τελευτῶντας δὲ κατὰ τὸ μέσον τῶν τεσσάρων Α, κινουμένους δὲ τούτους ὡς ἐπὶ τὸ ἔσχατον τοῦ 10 σταδίου τὸ Ε. διὸ καὶ πρῶτον λέγει τὸν κατὰ τὸ μέσον τῶν Α ὡς ἔμπροσθεν τῶν λοιπῶν ὄντα ἐν τῇ ἐπὶ τὸ Ε κινήσει. διὰ τοῦτο δὲ ἀρτίους ἔλαβε τοὺς ὄγκους, ἵνα ἔχωσιν ἥμισυ· δεῖται γὰρ τούτου, ὡς μαθησόμεθα. διὸ καὶ τὸ πρῶτον Β κατὰ τοῦ μέσου τῶν ἑστώτων Α τίθησιν, εἶτα καὶ ἄλλους ἴσους τῷ μεγέθει 15 καὶ τῷ ἀριθμῷ, τοῖς Β, δῆλον δὲ ὅτι καὶ τοῖς Α, λαμβάνει ἐφ᾽ ὧν τὰ Γ ἀντικινουμένους τοῖς Β. τῶν γὰρ Β ἀπὸ τοῦ μέσου τοῦ σταδίου, ἐν ᾧ καὶ τῶν Α τὸ μέσον ἦν, ἐπὶ τὸ ἔσχατον τοῦ σταδίου τὸ Ε κινουμένων οἱ Γ ἀπὸ τοῦ ἐσχάτου μέρους, ἐν ᾧ τὸ Ε, ἐπὶ τὸ Δ κινοῦνται τὸ ἐν τῇ ἀρχῇ τοῦ σταδίου, καὶ 20 πρῶτον δηλονότι τῶν τεσσάρων Γ ὁ πρὸς τὸ Δ νενευκώς, ἐφ᾽ ὃ ἡ κίνησις τοῖς Γ· τίθησιν δὲ τὸ πρῶτον Γ κατὰ τοῦ πρώτου Β. τοιαύτης οὖν τῆς ἐξ ἀρχῆς θέσεως ὑποτεθείσης ἐὰν τῶν Α ἑστώτων τὰ μὲν Β κινῆται ὡς ἀπὸ τοῦ μέσου τῶν τε Α καὶ τοῦ σταδίου ἐπὶ τὸ τέλος τοῦ σταδίου τὸ Ε, τὰ δὲ Γ ὡς ἀπὸ τοῦ ἐσχάτου τοῦ 25 σταδίου ἐπὶ τὴν ἀρχὴν δηλονότι (οὐ γὰρ δὴ ὡς "ἀπὸ τοῦ ἐσχάτου Β", ὅπερ ὡς ἔοικεν ἔν τισιν ἀντιγράφοις εὑρὼν ὁ Ἀλέξανδρος ἠναγκάσθη λέγειν, ὅτι ὃ πρότερον εἶπεν πρῶτον Β, τοῦτο νῦν ἔσχατον ἐκάλεσε), συμβαίνει τὸ πρῶτον Β ἅμα ἐπὶ τῷ ἐσχάτῳ εἶναι τῆς ἑαυτοῦ κινήσεως καὶ τὸ πρῶτον Γ, παρ᾽ ἄλληλα κινου-

suppose a stadium *DE*, and four bodies of equal size *AA*—or any
number, provided it be even, so that the number of bodies (or,

```
        ┌─────────────────────────┐
        │     A  A  A  A           │
   D    │  B  B  B  B  ───→        │   E
        │         ←───  C  C  C  C  │
        └─────────────────────────┘
```

as Eudemus calls them, cubes) has a half—which are stationary and
are placed so as to occupy a central stretch of the stadium. Of these
stationary bodies the "first" he defines as that nearest the beginning 5
of the stadium, on our diagram *D*, the last as that nearest *E*. And
he supposes four other bodies or cubes *BB* equal in size and number
to the stationary, originally stretching from the beginning of the
stadium to the middle of the four *A*s and moving towards the end
of the stadium *E*. And therefore he calls the *B* which is over against 10
the middle of the *A*s the "first" *B*, since it will be ahead of the others
in their motion towards *E*. The reason for supposing the number
of the bodies to be even is so that they should have a half: for this
is necessary to the argument, as we shall see. Accordingly he places
the first *B* over against the middle of the stationary *A*s, and then 15
supposes another row of bodies *CC* equal in size and number to the
*B*s, and therefore of course to the *A*s, and moving in the opposite
direction to the *B*s. For the *B*s move from the middle of the stadium,
which is also the mid-point of the *A*s, towards the end of the stadium
E, while the *C*s move from the end of the stadium, which we have 20
called *E*, towards the beginning of the stadium, *D* in our diagram,
and so clearly the "first" of the four *C*s is the one furthest advanced
towards *D*, in the direction of which the *C*s are moving, and the
first *C* is placed adjacent to the first *B*.

This then is the initial position. Then let the *A*s remain stationary, 25
and let the *B*s move from the middle of the *A*s and of the stadium
towards the end of the stadium *E*, and the *C*s from *the end of the
stadium* towards the beginning (this must clearly be the meaning,
and not *from the end B*, a reading which it seems that Alexander
found in some manuscripts, and was forced to adopt: for then what 30
he previously called the *first B* he has now called the *last*). Then it
results that the first *B* and the first *C* will "be at the end" of their

μένων αὐτῶν καὶ ἰσοταχῶς, ἢ ἐπὶ τῷ ἐσχάτῳ ἀλλήλων. τοῦ γὰρ
πρώτου Γ κατὰ τοῦ πρώτου Β ὄντος ἐξ ἀρχῆς, ἀντικινουμένων
αὐτῶν ἰσοταχῶς καὶ διεξελθόντων ἄλληλα, τὸ μὲν πρῶτον Β ἐπὶ
τῷ ἐσχάτῳ ἔσται Γ, τὸ δὲ πρῶτον Γ ἐπὶ τῷ ἐσχάτῳ Β. καὶ
5 τοῦτο ἂν εἴη τὸ συμβαίνειν τὸ πρῶτον Β ἅμα ἐπὶ τῷ ἐσχάτῳ
εἶναι καὶ τὸ πρῶτον Γ παρ' ἄλληλα κινουμένων· ἡ γὰρ παρ'
ἄλληλα κίνησις ποιεῖ τὸ ἐν τοῖς ἐσχάτοις ἀλλήλων γίνεσθαι.
συμβαίνει δέ, φησί, καὶ τὸ Γ, τὸ πρῶτον δηλονότι, παρὰ πάντα
τὰ Α διεληλυθέναι, τὸ δὲ Β παρὰ τὰ ἡμίση Α. καὶ ὅτι μὲν τὸ Β
10 τὸ ἀπὸ τοῦ μέσου τῶν Α ἀρχόμενον διὰ τῶν δύο Α ἐκινήθη ἢ διὰ
τῶν ἡμίσεων, ὁπόσα ἂν ᾖ ἄρτια, ἐν ὅσῳ τὸ Γ διὰ τῶν διπλασίων
Β δίεισι, δῆλον· τὸ γὰρ πρῶτον Β ἀπὸ τοῦ μέσου τῶν Α τὴν
ἀρχὴν ἐποιήσατο. καὶ ἐν ὅσῳ τὸ Β παρὰ τὰ δύο Α τὰ ἔσχατα τὰ
ἐστῶτα κινεῖται, τὸ Γ τὸ πρῶτον ἀντικινούμενον τοῖς Β διὰ τῶν
15 τεσσάρων Β δίεισιν· αἱ γὰρ δύο κινήσεις τῶν ἀντικινουμένων
διπλάσιον ἀνύουσι διάστημα τῆς μιᾶς, ἣν κινεῖται τὸ Β παρὰ τὰ
ἱστάμενα Α. καὶ τοῦτο μὲν δῆλον. πῶς δὲ τὸ Γ παρὰ πάντα τὰ Α
διελήλυθεν; οὔτε γὰρ παρὰ ταῦτα ἐκινεῖτο, ἀλλὰ παρὰ τὰ Β, οὔτε
ἀπ' ἀρχῆς τῶν Α ἐκινεῖτο, ἀλλὰ ἀπ' ἀρχῆς τῶν Β, ἥτις ἦν κατὰ
20 τὸ μέσον τῶν Α. ἢ ὅτι καὶ τὰ Β ἴσα ἦν τοῖς Α. τὸ οὖν Γ ἐν
ὅσῳ χρόνῳ παρὰ τὰ Β κεκίνηται, εἴη ἂν καὶ παρὰ τὰ Α τὰ ἴσα
τοῖς Β κεκινημένον. καὶ ὁ παραλογισμὸς ἐνταῦθά ἐστιν, ὅτι
ἔλαβεν ἁπλῶς ἐν ἴσῳ χρόνῳ κινούμενον τὸ παρὰ ἴσα κινούμενον
μὴ προσλογισάμενος, ὅτι τῶν ἴσων τὰ μὲν ἀντικινούμενα ἦν τὰ
25 δὲ ἐστῶτα. λαβὼν δὲ ὅμως, ὅτι ἐν ἴσῳ χρόνῳ τά τε Β καὶ τὰ Α
δίεισι τὰ Γ, ἐπειδὴ ἐν ὅσῳ χρόνῳ τὸ πρῶτον Β δίεισι τὰ δύο Α,
ἐν τοσούτῳ τὸ Γ τὰ τέσσαρα Β ἤτοι τὰ τέσσαρα Α, συνήγαγεν
ὅτι τὸ Β καίτοι ἰσοταχὲς ὂν τῷ Γ ἐν τῷ αὐτῷ χρόνῳ τὸ ἥμισυ
κινεῖται, οὗ τὸ Γ κινεῖται, ὅπερ ἐστὶ παρὰ τὰ προομολογηθέντα
30 καὶ τὰ ἐναργῆ· τὰ γὰρ ἰσοταχῆ ἐν ἴσῳ χρόνῳ τὸ ἴσον κινεῖται,

respective motions simultaneously "as they move past each other" with equal velocities. Or else we can interpret the phrase to mean that the first *B* will be opposite the last *C*, and vice-versa, at the same moment: for since the first *C* was to begin with adjacent to the first *B*, as the two rows move past each other in opposite directions and   5 with equal velocity, the first *B* will come opposite the last *C* and the first *C* opposite the last *B*. And this would be the meaning of saying that it results that "the first *B* and the first *C* will, as they move past one another, each be opposite the end simultaneously": for their movement past each other brings each opposite the end 10 body of the other row.

But it further results, he says, that "the *C*", that is, obviously, the first *C*, "has passed all the *A*s, but the ⟨first⟩ *B* has only passed half the *A*s". It is of course evident that the first *B*, starting from the mid-point of the *A*s, has moved past two *A*s or through half 15 whatever the even number of bodies chosen, while *C* has passed double the number of *B*s: for the first *B* was supposed to start from the middle of the *A*s. Also while *B* moves past the *two* end *A*s, which are stationary, the first *C*, moving in the opposite direction to the *B*s, has passed *four* *B*s: for the two contrary motions, taken together, 20 have the effect of doubling the distance of *B*'s motion, taken singly, past the stationary *A*s. So much is evident. But what is meant by saying that *C* has passed all the *A*s? For it was not past ⟨all⟩ the *A*s that it moved but past ⟨all⟩ the *B*s, nor did it move from the beginning of the *A*s but from the beginning of the *B*s, which was adjacent 25 to the middle of the *A*s. The reason must be because the *B*s also are equal to the *A*s. Therefore during the time in which the first *C* moved past the ⟨four⟩ *B*s it must have moved past ⟨four⟩ *A*s, since these are equal to the *B*s.

The fallacy lies in assuming without qualification that movements 30 past bodies of equal size take an equal time, without taking into account the further fact that of the equal bodies some are moving in opposite directions and some are stationary. None the less he makes the assumption that the *C*s take an equal time to pass the *B*s and the *A*s and concludes that since, during the time which the first *B* takes 35 to pass two *A*s, the first *C* has passed four *B*s *or* four *A*s, the first *B*, though its velocity is the same as that of the first *C*, yet moves only half the distance the first *C* moves in the same time—which is in accordance neither with the presuppositions of the argument nor with common sense: for bodies moving with an equal velocity cover 40

ἀλλ' ὅταν ὁμοίως ἔχῃ, ὥστε ἢ ἄμφω παρὰ τὰ ἑστῶτα κινεῖσθαι,
ἢ ἄμφω παρὰ τὰ κινούμενα, καὶ οὐχ ὅταν τὰ μὲν παρὰ τὰ ἑστῶτα
ὡς τὸ Β, τὰ δὲ παρὰ τὰ ἀντικινούμενα ὡς τὸ Γ. ἔτι δὲ καὶ ὁ
χρόνος, ἐν ᾧ κινεῖται τὸ Β διὰ τῶν δύο Α, ἥμισύς ἐστι τοῦ
5 χρόνου, ἐν ᾧ κινεῖται τὸ Γ διὰ τῶν τεσσάρων Β, εἴπερ ἴσα τὰ Α
τοῖς Β, καὶ ἰσοταχῆ τό τε Β καὶ τὸ Γ. ἐδόκει δὲ καὶ ἴσος εἶναι
ὁ χρόνος ἤτοι ὁ αὐτός, ἐν ᾧ τὸ Β ἐκινεῖτο διὰ τῶν δύο Α, καὶ ἐν
ᾧ τὸ Γ διὰ τῶν τεσσάρων Β. συμβήσεται οὖν καὶ μέγεθος τὸ
αὐτὸ εἶναι διπλάσιόν τε καὶ ἥμισυ, εἴπερ ἐν τῷ αὐτῷ χρόνῳ τῶν
10 ἰσοταχῶν τὸ μὲν Β τὰ δύο Α διῄει, τὸ δὲ Γ τὰ τέσσαρα Β, ἴσων
ὄντων τῶν Β τοῖς Α· καὶ χρόνον τὸν αὐτὸν διπλάσιόν τε καὶ
ἥμισυν, εἴπερ καὶ ἥμισυς ἦν ὁ χρόνος, ἐν ᾧ τὸ Β διὰ τῶν δύο Α
διῄει, τοῦ χρόνου, ἐν ᾧ τὸ Γ διὰ τῶν τεσσάρων Β, καὶ ὁ αὐτός.
τὸ δὲ ἴσον γὰρ ἑκάτερόν ἐστι παρ' ἕκαστον δηλοῖ ὅτι καὶ τὸ Β
15 καὶ τὸ Γ ἰσοταχῆ ὄντα ἴσον χρόνον ποιεῖ παρ' ἕκαστον, δι' ὧν
κινεῖται τῶν τε Β καὶ τῶν Α. εἰ δὲ ἴσον, δῆλον ὅτι διπλάσιός
ἐστιν ὁ χρόνος, ἐν ᾧ τὸ Γ τὰ τέσσαρα Β δίεισιν, ἥμισυς δέ, ἐν ᾧ
τὸ Β τὰ δύο Α, ἢ μᾶλλον, ἐν ᾧ τὸ Γ τὰ τέσσαρα Α δίεισι, τοῦ ἐν
ᾧ τὸ Β τὸ ἰσοταχὲς αὐτῷ τὰ δύο Α. εἴρηται γάρ, ὅτι ἐν ᾧ τὰ Β
20 δίεισι τὸ Γ, ἐν τούτῳ καὶ τὰ Α.

an equal distance in an equal time, but only when their relative
circumstances are the same and either both are moving past stationary
bodies or both past moving, but not when some are moving past
stationary bodies (like B) and some past bodies moving in an
opposite direction (like C). Further, the time taken by B to pass 5
two As is half the time taken by C to pass four Bs, if the As are equal
to the Bs and B and C move with equal velocity. But the time in
which B passes two As and that in which C passes four Bs are
supposed to be equal or the same. It follows therefore *both* that the
same magnitude is double and half, since in the same time of two 10
bodies moving with equal velocity B passes two As and C passes
four Bs, though the Bs are equal in size to the As: *and* that the same
time is both double and half, if the time taken by B to pass two As
is both half and the same as the time C took to pass four Bs.

The phrase "each takes an equal time to pass each body" means 15
that B and C, since they move with equal velocity, take an equal
time in passing both each B and each A. But if this is so, then it is
clear that the time taken by C to pass four Bs is double that taken
by B to pass two As, or rather that the time which C takes to pass
four As is double that which B, though moving with a velocity 20
equal to C's, takes to pass two As: for as was said the time C takes
to pass the Bs, it will also take to pass the As.

MOTION

§ A

My reason for inserting these two passages at this point I have already given (cf. p. 38 above, my preliminary remarks on the τόπος argument). The argument contained in them is again too general in form for us to be able to tell whether it formed part of any particular polemic. The argument itself is quite clear from the two passages. If a thing is moving it must be moving either in the place where it *is* or in the place where it *is not*.

But (1) the second alternative is absurd;
    (2) a body, if it is in a given place, must be at rest.

Therefore a body which is moving must be at rest.

With (2) above cf. the third argument on motion, "the flying arrow".

Sextus Empiricus, *Pyrrh. Hyp.* III. 71, quotes this argument from Diodorus Kronos, who presumably took it from Zeno. His version is as follows: εἰ κινεῖταί τι, ἤτοι ἐν ᾧ ἔστι τόπῳ κινεῖται ἢ ἐν ᾧ οὐκ ἔστιν. οὔτε δὲ ἐν ᾧ ἔστι· μένει γὰρ ἐν αὐτῷ, εἴπερ ἐν αὐτῷ ἔστιν· οὔτε ἐν ᾧ μὴ ἔστιν· ὅπου γάρ τι μὴ ἔστιν, ἐκεῖ οὐδὲ δρᾶσαί τι οὐδὲ παθεῖν δύναται. οὐκ ἄρα κινεῖταί τι.

§ B

We come now to the four famous arguments on motion, by which Zeno is most generally and widely known, and with which the great majority of literature about him is concerned. Against whom were they originally directed, if against anyone in particular?

We have seen that there is reason to believe that the arguments on plurality were directed against the Pythagoreans. That is to say, they show to be self-contradictory and absurd a certain set of presuppositions which it seems likely that the Pythagoreans held; the kind of pluralism which Zeno is attacking bears a strong resemblance to the kind of pluralism taught by the Pythagoreans. On the other hand the arguments on "place", and on "place and motion", are too general for us to be able to say against whom they are directed. The presuppositions Zeno is there attempting to discredit are rather those of common sense than of any particular school. He is simply trying to show that there are inherent contradictions in the notions of place and of motion; and it does not seem that any particular theory of space or motion is the object of his attack, but rather the ordinary common-sense ideas of them. These arguments on place, and place and motion, *may* of course have formed part of an attack on Pythagoreanism: but there does not seem to be any conclusive reason for believing that they actually did. And there was no need for Zeno to have confined his attacks to the Pythagoreans. The presuppositions of common sense are quite as opposed to a Parmenidean monism as are those of Pythagorean pluralism: and it was equally in Zeno's interest to discredit both.

This reasoning is applicable also to the four arguments on motion. There is no *a priori* need to suppose them to have been directed against any one school in particular; more especially as the evident facts of motion are what seem to ordinary common sense to conflict most radically with Parmenides's monism. On the other hand if an examination of the arguments themselves shows that a particular theory of motion is being attacked, we can then proceed to ask whether there is any evidence to show whose this theory was. But a consideration of this question must be postponed until the arguments themselves have been examined.

A word must first be said of Zeno's more general purpose in these arguments. I take the conventional view, that Parmenides had declared all plurality and motion to be in some way or other illusory; and that Zeno's arguments were intended to give support to Parmenides's thesis by showing that the obvious facts of plurality and motion, which seem so clearly to conflict with it, themselves cannot be accounted for without contradiction. This was Plato's opinion and I see no reason to doubt it. Aristotle and the commentators confirm it. Aristotle in general refers to Zeno as trying to prove "that motion is impossible" (cf. passage No. 19, p. 42, l. 7; 65b 18 τὸν Ζήνωνος λόγον...ὡς οὐκ ἔστι κινεῖσθαι; 179b 20, 160b 7): and the commentators speak of him as trying ἀναιρεῖν τὴν κίνησιν.[1] This is a natural way for them to speak if they assumed, like Plato, that Zeno was trying to show that the

---

[1] Cf. passage No. 21, Philoponus; passage No. 22, Themistius; Simp. *Phys.* 1012. 35 for the same phrase; cf. also Alexander, *Met.* 334. 13.

idea of motion is inherently contradictory. Motion like plurality had to be shown to be illusory if the Parmenidean one was to be accepted. And this and this only is the ultimate object of Zeno's arguments.

I have thought it worth while to emphasise this because it has been denied by Milhaud[1] and by Tannery.[2] Their arguments do not seem to me to be at all convincing, and I prefer to follow Brochard, to whom I refer for a defence of the conventional view against them.[3]

THE DICHOTOMY

Generally so called because Zeno in it argues from the possibility of halving any given distance infinitely. Aristotle refers to it as ἡ διχοτομία (p. 50, l. 8), "the dichotomy argument".

19. p. 42, l. 6. τέτταρες. Simplicius (1012. 27) does not seem to know whether Aristotle quotes four arguments because there were only four, or because these were the four πραγματειωδέστεροι. Aristotle's own language (p. 42, l. 6) is ambiguous on the point. In § A of these passages on motion (Nos. 17 and 18) I have already quoted an argument about motion different from any of the four now in question: so it certainly seems as if there were other arguments of Zeno on motion besides these four.[4] On the other hand there is, as we shall see, a definite connexion between the arguments, and so it looks as if Aristotle's choice had not been merely arbitrary. Perhaps the arguments did actually form a tetralogy in Zeno's book, and Aristotle selected them from among others as having "given the most trouble".

---

[1] *Rev. Mét. et Mor.* I. 1893, pp. 151–6 and 400–6.

[2] *Science Hellène*, chapters on Parmenides and Zeno.

[3] *Rev. Mét. et Mor.* I. 1893, pp. 208 ff. Also published in his *Études de Philosophie Ancienne et Moderne.*

[4] Elias in *Categ.* p. 109. 6 Busse, Diels, 19. A. 15, mentions five; and we have of course five extant. But there may have been more. The passage is worth quoting because it contains Antisthenes the Cynic's comment on Zeno's arguments: καί ποτε πάλιν τῷ αὐτῷ συνηγορῶν διδασκάλῳ ἀκίνητον λέγοντι τὸ ὄν, διὰ πέντε ἐπιχειρημάτων κατασκευάζει, ὅτι ἀκίνητον τὸ ὄν· οἷς ἀντειπεῖν μὴ δυνηθεὶς Ἀντισθένης ὁ Κυνικὸς ἀναστὰς ἐβάδισε, νομίσας ἰσχυροτέραν εἶναι πάσης τῆς διὰ λόγων ἀντιλογίας τὴν διὰ τῆς ἐνεργείας ἀπόδειξιν.

p. 42, l. 8. διὰ τὸ πρότερον εἰς τὸ ἥμισυ, i.e. the argument is, in outline, that a moving body in completing any given distance would have to pass through an infinite number of half-way points; which is impossible, and therefore motion is impossible. If we call the straight line *AB* the given distance, there are two possibilities between which Aristotle's language is ambiguous:

$$A \vdash\!\!+\!\!+\!\!-\!\!+\!\!-\!\!-\!\!-\!\!-\!\!-\!\!+\!\!-\!\!-\!\!-\!\!-\!\!-\!\!+\!\!-\!\!+\!\!+\!\! \dashv B$$

The infinite number of half-way points may either be the series $a, a^1, a^{11}, a^{111}, \ldots$, or else the series $a, a^1, a^2, a^3, \ldots$. The commentators are unanimous in taking the first alternative: see below, note to p. 44, ll. 6–7.

p. 42, l. 11. ἅψασθαι τῶν ἀπείρων. The rather indefinite Greek neuter is always difficult to translate. I have tried where τὸ ἄπειρον and τὰ ἄπειρα occur in these passages to make the English more definite and bring out the essential meaning of the Greek. Thus τῶν ἀπείρων ἅψασθαι I have translated by "to make an infinite number of contacts": τὰ ἄπειρα διελθεῖν (as e.g. at p. 44, ll. 9–10) by "to traverse an infinite number of positions".

p. 42, l. 12. ἐν πεπερασμένῳ χρόνῳ. This seems to form an essential part of the first argument as Zeno propounded it, and reappears in the commentaries both of Simplicius and Philoponus. And Aristotle's answer to Zeno, contained in the second of the two passages in No. 19, consists in saying that space and time are both infinitely divisible and that therefore there is no asymmetry; which implies that some reference to time was an essential in Zeno's argument.

We may therefore assume that Zeno's argument turned, in Aristotle's words, on the impossibility of making an infinite number of contacts in a finite time, and may reconstruct it as follows:

(1) Since the continuum, space, is infinitely divisible, there must be in any given distance an infinite number of half-way points (cf. note above, *ad* p. 42, l. 8, and below, *ad* p. 44, ll. 6–7). And a body traversing this given distance must reach each one of these half-way points in turn.

(2) Now though the distances traversed to reach each succeeding point are diminishing infinitely in a constant ratio of 2 : 1, yet each point must be reached a finite time after the last.

(3) But these finite intervals of time must be infinite in number: and therefore the sum of them must be infinite.

(4) It is therefore impossible to traverse the given distance in a finite time.

And since the same argument will hold good of *any* finite distance, we can conclude that it is impossible to traverse any distance (however small) in a finite time (however long), and therefore that motion is impossible.

We have thus made the argument turn on the requisite impossibility. You cannot make an infinite number of contacts (sc. with the successive middle-points) one after another in a finite time. The argument clearly assumes the infinite divisibility of space. Probably also that of time: for the finite times of step (2) are probably assumed to diminish as the space to be traversed diminishes. But this point is not really essential to the argument, which turns simply on the impossibility of covering the *infinite* number of distances contained in any finite distance in a *finite* time.

p. 42, l. 14. κατὰ ποσόν. An inaccurate expression: it is *quantitative* in either case. Aristotle must here intend κατὰ ποσόν to be taken in antithesis to κατὰ διαίρεσιν at p. 42, l. 15 (cf. ἤτοι κατὰ διαίρεσιν ἢ τοῖς ἐσχάτοις, p. 42, ll. 13–14), i.e. as equivalent to κατὰ πρόσθεσιν (cf. *Phys.* Γ 204 a 6–7, where this antithesis is stated).

20. p. 44, l. 2. ἐν πεπερασμένῳ ἄπειρα διεξιέναι expresses the same essential point as Aristotle's ἀπείρων ἅψασθαι.

p. 44, l. 2. διεξιέναι. In what follows I have tried to keep the distinction between διεξιέναι and διιέναι by translating the former "to complete" (the combination of διά and ἐξ suggesting moving *through* and coming *out at the end of*), the latter "to traverse". But the distinction does not seem important for the essential meaning of the passage.

p. 44, l. 3. τὸ συνημμένον, "his hypothesis", i.e. the statement made in the clause εἰ ἔστι κίνησις...διεξιέναι. On the use of συνημμένον as a technical term *v.* on p. 42, l. 18 below.

p. 44, ll. 6–7. πρὸ τοῦ ἡμίσεος ὅλου τὸ ἐκείνου ἥμισυ. We have already seen that Aristotle's words are ambiguous between two methods of constructing the infinite series of points required by the argument. Simplicius and Philoponus are both unambiguous. The construction they give is quite clear, and may be represented diagrammatically thus:

$$A \mid\!\!\underset{a^3\ a^2}{\mid\,\mid}\quad\underset{a^1}{\mid}\qquad\underset{a}{\mid}\qquad\qquad\qquad\qquad\qquad\mid B$$

where a, a^1, a^2, a^3 are the successive half-way points which the construction gives.

p. 44, ll. 11–12. λέγων ἀδύνατον εἶναι, sc. in the second passage quoted in No.19, *Phys.* Z 233 a 21ff. Notice Simplicius's insistence on the reference to time in this argument. The version he gives in this first passage fits very well with the reconstruction I have given on p. 67.

p. 44, l. 17. ἁπτόμενον αὐτῶν ἑκάστου, "making an infinite number of contacts *one by one*". The point of this I have tried to express in other words in my step (2) (p. 67 above). The contacts must be made *one by one*, i.e. each successive half-way point must be reached a finite time after its predecessor.

The point is further brought out (1) at ll. 23–5 ἅψασθαι...αὐτά, and (2) more explicitly still at ll. 28–30 καὶ ἐκ τοῦ μὴ δυνατὸν... μερῶν.

(1) Here Simplicius notes that it is essential to suppose the positions are reached and the contacts made one by one, i.e. each one at a definite interval after its predecessor. A body must be supposed to move "along and through" a given distance (κινού-μενον καὶ διὸν ὁτιοῦν μέγεθος p. 44, l. 21), and so "along and through" the infinite number of positions given by the construction, thus "making an infinite number of contacts" as it touches one by one the infinite number of half-way points constructed. It cannot be supposed in any way to pass along the line without making contact with these points, by stepping over them as it were and missing them out (this seems the force of ὑπερβαίνειν: a rather loose and figurative expression).

(2) Here Simplicius definitely says that the successive points given by the construction are each reached at a definite interval after its predecessor (ἐν ἄλλῳ καὶ ἄλλῳ τοῦ χρόνου, "at successive moments of time"). The intervals would presumably be supposed to decrease with the distance (there is no reference to any atomic view of time here, such as we shall find in the "arrow" and the

"stadium"): but the important point is that there is a definite interval of time between the reaching of one half-way point and the next.

And this, I take it, is also the reason for the introduction by Simplicius of the metaphor of counting in the last line: for we count one number *after* another (cf. *De Lin. Insec.* 969 *b* 3 τὸ γὰρ ἀριθμεῖν ἐστι τὸ μετὰ ἐπιστάσεως), and so have in the number-series also a series which is infinite, and whose terms are each reached a finite time after its predecessor. The number-series with its infinite number of terms each reached after a finite interval is thus introduced by Simplicius as an analogy to the infinite series of points, each reached after a finite interval, given by the construction. The metaphor is, however, not really in place in this form of the argument, but in the other form (not due to Zeno himself) given in passages Nos. 23 and 24 below. I take it to be an addition of Simplicius's own here, made in order to elucidate the argument in the way I have described, and no doubt suggested to him by the other form of the argument. In this other form of the argument the idea of counting is an integral part of the reasoning, and not, as here, an analogy used in explanation, and is used to the exclusion of the time reference and not in illustration of it (see notes *ad loc.*).

An interesting point may be raised here. On Simplicius's view of the construction which yields the infinite series the body can never as a matter of fact be supposed to move at all. For his construction yields no first point for the body to move to, as can be seen by a glance at the diagrams above; and so there seems to be no sense in talking about it reaching each successive point after a definite time interval. On the other hand, if we adopt the other construction

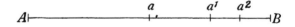

then we suppose that the body first moves to *a*, then to *a*¹, then to *a*², and so on. Aristotle's own language we have seen to be ambiguous on this point: and as Simplicius does not seem to have known much, if anything, of the argument apart from what he knew from Aristotle, I think he may very well be mistaken here. Certainly the other construction seems to give better sense, and would suit Zeno equally well. For with it also there follows the conclusion that it is impossible to traverse any finite distance in a finite time.

Of course in strict logic it will follow from this construction as much as from the other that a body at *A* can in fact never move from *A*. For the argument that applies to *AB* applies equally to any and every distance taken from *A*. But this construction will yield a point *a* which *for the sake of the argument* can be supposed to be the first point reached by the body in its movement along *AB*, even though the argument subsequently shows that it is logically impossible for the point *a*, or any other point, ever to be reached.

p. 44, l. 18. συνημμένον, "his hypothesis", i.e. what is expressed in the clause εἰ ἔστι κίνησις...ἁπτόμενον αὐτῶν ἑκάστου p. 44, ll. 16–17. Liddell and Scott (8th ed.) s.v. συνάπτω III. 3 give τὸ συνημμένον=a hypothetical *syllogism*. This translation is wrong. συνημμένον means a hypothetical *proposition*, e.g. in the example given by L. and S. themselves from Sext. Emp. *M.* 8. 109, εἴπερ ἡμέρα ἐστί, φῶς ἐστι: for definitions of this sense of the word *v.* Sext. Emp. *loc. cit.*, Aul. Gell. XVI. 8, 9, Diog. Laert. VII. 80. An hypothetical *syllogism* is an argument in syllogistic form of which at least one premiss is hypothetical: for the forms of hypothetical syllogism cf. Diog. Laert. VII. 80–2 (of modern logicians cf. Joseph, *Introduction to Logic*, pp. 339 ff., who denies that this form of reasoning is strictly syllogistic, and Keynes, *Formal Logic*, pp. 300 ff.).

The whole argument as stated by Simplicius at p. 44, ll. 16–18 is in the form of a hypothetical syllogism. Diogenes describes this particular form as follows (*loc. cit.*): δεύτερος δ᾽ ἐστὶν...ὁ διὰ συνημμένου καὶ τοῦ ἀντικειμένου τοῦ λήγοντος τὸ ἀντικείμενον τοῦ ἡγουμένου ἔχων συμπέρασμα, οἷον, εἰ ἡμέρα ἐστί, φῶς ἐστι· ἀλλὰ νύξ ἐστι· οὐκ ἄρα ἡμέρα ἐστί. ἡ γὰρ πρόσληψις γίνεται ἐκ τοῦ ἀντικειμένου τῷ λήγοντι καὶ ἡ ἐπιφορὰ ἐκ τοῦ ἀντικειμένου τῷ ἡγουμένῳ. From this the various parts of the argument and their technical terms should be clear. The conditional clause as a whole is called τὸ συνημμένον: and is divided into two members, the condition, τὸ ἡγούμενον (here εἰ ἡμέρα ἐστί) and the contingent clause, τὸ λῆγον (here φῶς ἐστι).[1] The minor premiss (ἀλλὰ νύξ ἐστι) is called ἡ πρόσληψις, and the conclusion ἡ ἐπιφορά. In the present context two of these terms occur, συνημμένον at p. 44, l. 18 and πρόσληψις at p. 44, l. 26, where I have duly translated it "minor

[1] Cf. Arnold, *Roman Stoicism*, ch. VI, § 162.

premiss" (L. and S. give this meaning correctly s.v.). The συνημμένον of the argument as stated by Simplicius in ll. 16–18 is as I have
said, and, as can now be seen from the definition of terms given, the
clause εἰ ἔστι κίνησις...ἁπτόμενον αὐτῶν ἑκάστου p. 44, ll. 16–17:
the πρόσληψις is the clause ἀλλὰ μὴν τοῦτο ἀδύνατον p. 44, ll. 17–
18. And the correctness of Simplicius's use of this terminology can be
seen from the fact that ll. 19–25 do as a matter of fact give the proof
of the statement contained in the clause εἰ ἔστι κίνησις...ἑκάστου,
and ll. 26 ff. give the proof of the statement ἀλλὰ...ἀδύνατον.

The whole terminology is that of later Stoic logic.

p. 44, l. 28. ἀδιεξίτητον, interminable, such that you never come
to the *end* of it (cf. the translation of διεξίέναι by "to complete").
In modern language a series with no last term.

p. 44, l. 32. ἀριθμῆσαι δὲ ἀδύνατον..., because there is no last
term to such series. Cf. also above, p. 70 and below, *ad* No. 23.

21. There is very little that calls for fresh comment in either of
these two passages. The commentary is less full than that of Simplicius, and no essentially new point is introduced.

p. 46, l. 5. σημεῖα, points. The geometrical term. Zeno's
argument is essentially geometrical in origin, and we should beware
when speaking of it of using phraseology about series drawn from
modern arithmetic.

p. 46, l. 8. ὅτι δὲ.... Recalls the ultimate object of Zeno's
polemic—to support the Parmenidean "one".

p. 46, l. 10. πρὶν τὴν ὅλην.... The same construction as that
given by Simplicius, *v.* above.

p. 46, ll. 15–16. πᾶσα δὲ...κινεῖται. Cf. step (4) of my version
of the argument, p. 68.

p. 46, l. 18. ἀδιεξίτητον. Cf. note on p. 44, l. 28.

22. Again adds nothing essential and calls for no fresh comment.

p. 46, ll. 23–4. ὁ δὲ χρόνος...πεπερασμένος. If motion through
a finite distance (Themistius instances τὸ ποδιαῖον l. 22) is to take
place, it must take place in a finite time: but this is impossible because
of the infinite divisibility of any distance. Again the argument turns
on the impossibility of covering in a finite time the infinite number
of distances contained in any finite distance.

23. We have here a further statement by Aristotle of Zeno's argument. (1) The first part of the statement, $\epsilon i \; \grave{\alpha} \epsilon i \ldots \delta\iota\epsilon\xi\epsilon\lambda\theta\epsilon\hat{\iota}\nu$ p. 46, l. 26–p. 48, l. 1, clearly re-states, without variation, the argument as we have already met it.

p. 48, l. 1. $\tau\grave{\alpha} \; \delta' \; \check{\alpha}\pi\epsilon\iota\rho\alpha \; \grave{\alpha}\delta\acute{\upsilon}\nu\alpha\tau\upsilon\nu \; \delta\iota\epsilon\xi\epsilon\lambda\theta\epsilon\hat{\iota}\nu$. "It is impossible to complete an infinite number of distances." I have translated thus because Aristotle seems to have in mind here rather the infinite number of half-way distances to be completed than the infinite number of half-way positions to be occupied. A difference of point of view which does not affect the essentials of the argument.

(2) p. 48, l. 1. $\check{\eta} \; \dot{\omega}s \; \tau\grave{\omega}\nu \; \alpha\dot{\upsilon}\tau\grave{\omega}\nu \ldots$ Aristotle seems here to imply two things. (a) That this form of the argument was not due to Zeno. But he gives no indication to whom it is to be attributed. It seems most natura to assume that some pupil of Zeno or some younger Eleatic was responsible for it. (b) On the other hand Aristotle clearly implies that this is merely a new form of the argument and that the reasoning is essentially the same.

p. 48, l. 3. $\dot{\alpha}\rho\iota\theta\mu\epsilon\hat{\iota}\nu$. The novelty in this form of the argument consists in the introduction of the idea of *counting*. We have already seen Simplicius introducing this idea in his elucidation of the argument. But from what Aristotle says here it is clear that in the argument as originally formulated by Zeno there was no explicit reference to counting or to the infinity of the number-series. And my formulation of the argument fulfills this condition.

Simplicius (p. 44, ll. 28 ff.) introduced the analogy of counting when explaining that the moving object must reach each successive half-way point at a finite time interval after its predecessor. And I therefore suggested that the reason for introducing the analogy was that, as in counting we reach (as it were) each number *after* the one before it, we have in the number-series another infinite series each term of which is reached a finite time after its predecessor.

But in the other formulation of the argument which Aristotle gives here there is no reference to time; the proof depends simply on the infinity of the number-series. For let us suppose an object X moving along the line AB and reaching successively the half-way points a, a^1, a^2, and so on.

Then theoretically an observer watching the progress of X along AB should be able to count the half-way points as X passes them. But *ex hypothesi* the number of half-way points is infinite: and

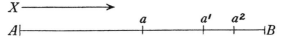

ex hypothesi it is impossible to count an infinite number. Yet if the complete distance AB is ever to be traversed the observer would have to have counted an infinite number since the number of half-way points is infinite. We conclude therefore that it is impossible for X to traverse AB, and so for any body to traverse any distance.

The conclusion is the same as that of the form of the argument used by Zeno: and it makes use of the same principle of infinite dichotomy. Hence Aristotle can regard the reasoning as essentially the same in both forms of the argument. But this second form argues from the infinity of the number of the terms in the series given by successive dichotomies and from the impossibility of counting such an infinite number, and not from the impossibility of covering the infinite number of resultant distances in a finite time.

24. Falls naturally into two parts: that explaining the first, and that explaining the second form of the argument. The explanation is in each case clear and calls for little comment.

p. 48, ll. 12–13. ἐν τῷ συνημμένῳ, "his hypothesis", i.e. the statement εἰ ἔστι κίνησις...διεληλυθός, ll. 7–8, the opposite of which is here assumed. For whereas the hypothesis assumes that "if there is motion there will be something which has traversed an infinite number of positions in a finite time", the assumption here made is that "it is *impossible* to get to the end of an infinite number of positions in a finite time", i.e. an assumption opposite to that made in the hypothesis.

On the technical term συνημμένον v. note *ad* p. 44, l. 18 above.

p. 48, ll. 14-15. διότι...τὰ ἄπειρα. We have seen that this has a more important place in the second form of the argument. It is, of course, a necessary presupposition of the first form (cf. stages 3 and 4, p. 68 above): but the argument does not turn on it in the same way. I think it is rather part of Simplicius's explanation here than of Zeno's actual argument.

p. 48, ll. 20–1. ἔσται ὁ ἀριθμῶν...τὰ ἄπειρα. This brings out very clearly the point that the second form of the argument turns simply on the infinity of the number-series, on the impossibility of "counting an infinite number". And this is the point I have tried to bring out in my own explanation of the argument, which is thus supported by Simplicius.

25. The interest and importance of this passage does not lie in any light it throws on Zeno's own views. It merely states briefly the argument as he originally framed it with the time reference. And I have no comment to make on it from this standpoint.

Its interest lies rather in the connexion made between the arguments of Zeno and the belief in ἄτομοι γραμμαί. This doctrine was certainly held by Xenocrates (cf. Simp. 138. 14, 140. 12, 142. 16) and possibly by Plato (cf. *Met.* A, 992a 20 and Ross's note *ad loc.*); and according to this passage part at any rate of its purpose was to answer this argument of Zeno. We may also compare *Phys.* A, 187a 1–4 ἔνιοι δ᾽ ἐνέδοσαν τοῖς λόγοις ἀμφοτέροις, τῷ μὲν ὅτι πάντα ἕν, εἰ τὸ ὂν ἓν σημαίνει, ὅτι ἔστι τὸ μὴ ὄν, τῷ δὲ ἐκ τῆς διχοτομίας, ἄτομα ποιήσαντες μεγέθη. In the second of these λόγοι (ὁ ἐκ τῆς διχοτομίας) Alexander (referred to by Simplicius, 138. 3 ff.) sees a reference to Zeno's arguments against plurality.[1] Probably the supporters of the ἄτομοι γραμμαί were trying to answer Zeno's attack on plurality (for as we have seen the plurality he was attacking, with its point-unit element, was definitely mathematical in character) quite as much as they were trying to answer the first argument on motion. Aristotle's words at 187a 3, τῷ ἐκ τῆς διχοτομίας, might refer to either, since both argue from infinite divisibility.

Of the doctrine of ἄτομοι γραμμαί Ross (*Met.* I. p. 206) writes: "The doctrine of indivisible lines may have been adopted as if it were the only alternative to the Pythagorean construction of the line out of points." It was of course Zeno's attacks that had shown the "construction of the line out of points" to be an impossibility. And his historical position between the Pythagoreans and Xenocrates (and perhaps Plato) is thus clear.

[1] Cf. on No. 2, p. 22 above.

THE ACHILLES

26. p. 50, l. 1. ὁ καλούμενος Ἀχιλλεύς. Cf. Simplicius, l. 16 below. "The argument is called the Achilles because of the introduction into it of Achilles, who, the argument says, cannot possibly overtake the tortoise he is pursuing." The tortoise does not appear in Aristotle's version, which has only τὸ βραδύτατον ll. 2, 4, 11, though Achilles, referred to also as τὸ τάχιστον ll. 2, 10, does.

This and the two following arguments are given by Aristotle only in the passages from *Phys.* Z quoted, and not referred to by him elsewhere.

p. 50, ll. 3–4. ἔμπροσθεν...τὸ βραδύτερον. This gives the kernel of the argument. If Achilles gives the tortoise a start, he must first, as he runs after it, reach the point from which the tortoise started. By that time the tortoise will have progressed a certain distance from its starting-point. And Achilles must again reach this point before he can overtake it. But while he is doing this the tortoise will have progressed still further—and so on *ad infinitum*.

p. 50, ll. 5–6. ἐν τῷ διαιρεῖν μὴ δίχα. As Aristotle points out, p. 50, ll. 4–5, 8–9, in both this and the previous argument Zeno is arguing from the infinite divisibility of space. Only this argument differs from the other in that here the process of division is not one of dichotomy. The successive subdivisions stand to each other not in the ratio of $\frac{1}{2}$ but of $\frac{\text{tortoise's speed}}{\text{Achilles's speed}}$. An example Simplicius gives at 1014. 23 makes the argument quite clear. Suppose a stadium in which Achilles and the tortoise are running a race. Suppose

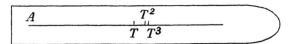

Achilles starts at A and the tortoise at T; and suppose that Achilles runs ten times as fast as the tortoise. Then by the time Achilles has reached the point T, the tortoise will have reached a point T^2, at a distance $\frac{AT}{10}$ from T, since the tortoise only goes $\frac{1}{10}$ the distance Achilles goes in the same time. Similarly, by the time Achilles has reached the point T^2 from T, the tortoise will have reached a point T^3, at a distance $\dfrac{TT^2}{10}$ from T^2. And so on *ad infinitum*. This is the argument. Its conclusion, as Simplicius points out (ll. 14–15), is that Achilles will never catch the tortoise, which is absurd; and therefore motion is an impossibility. And it proceeds quite clearly on the assumption that space and time are divisible *ad infinitum*.

The following quotation from Prof. Broad ("Note on Achilles and the tortoise", *Mind*, N.S. xxii. p. 319) summarises the argument neatly. "The supporter of the Achilles can prove that if they ⟨sc. Achilles and the tortoise⟩ meet at any point, it must be beyond every point given by the construction. He can also prove that the number of points given by the construction is infinite. And now he assumes the plausible proposition 'What is beyond every one of a series of infinite points must be infinitely beyond the first point of the series.' If this were true his conclusion would follow, for it would take the two an infinite time to reach the only point at which they could possibly meet. But the proposition is utterly false."

p. 50, l. 10. τετραγῳδημένον, "a dramatic effect is produced". The Oxf. Trans. renders "even the quickest runner in legendary tradition etc."

The first translation has more point. For the introduction of Achilles and the tortoise in this, of the flying arrow in the next argument, and of the stadium in the last give them a certain vivid and dramatic quality, of which Aristotle evidently thoroughly disapproved, but which seems to have been very characteristic of Zeno's reasoning.

Cf. L. and S. s.vv. τραγῳδεῖν, τραγῳδία for the meaning "pompous", "bombastic" conveyed by these words. So in more journalistic modern English *dramatic* is used of events to mean "sensational", of actions to mean "done for effect" (cf. melodramatic). I have used it here as the nearest English parallel.

27. I have already commented on p. 50, ll. 14 ff. and p. 50, ll. 16 ff. In the rest of this passage Simplicius is paraphrasing and expanding Aristotle's very compressed account of the argument. His paraphrase is very clear; and I have followed it closely in my account of the argument above. It brings out very well the point that Achilles can never be level with the tortoise at any point given by Zeno's construction.

Of the other two commentators, Philoponus has nothing on the Achilles, and Themistius adds nothing new. He has the same example as Simplicius (*v.* above, p. 76), which was evidently a stock one. I have accordingly not quoted him.

THE ARROW

More properly "the flying arrow", $\dot{\eta}$ $\dot{o}\iota\sigma\tau\dot{o}s$ $\phi\epsilon\rho o\mu\acute{e}\nu\eta$ (p. 52, l. 1). Simplicius and Philoponus call it $\tau\dot{o}$ $\phi\epsilon\rho\acute{o}\mu\epsilon\nu o\nu$ $\beta\acute{e}\lambda os$, $\beta\acute{e}\lambda os$ meaning any missile weapon and not arrow specifically. I have accordingly, to mark the distinction, rendered $\beta\acute{e}\lambda os$ by "missile", though this is somewhat clumsy in English.

28. p. 52, l. 2. $\dot{\epsilon}\kappa$ $\tau\hat{\omega}\nu$ $\nu\hat{\nu}\nu$. The view that time is composed of instants as atomic minimal parts. This, Aristotle points out, is the necessary presupposition for the argument. And in this it is contrasted with the previous two, which both presuppose the infinite divisibility of space and time.

On this view of time motion also must be discontinuous; for a motion from A to B must consist of a series of positions $x, x^1, x^2, \ldots$ occupied by the moving body at the series of instants which make up the time occupied by its motion. And so a natural consequence of this view would be to regard space also as discontinuous and made up (so to speak) of positions (cf. the fourth argument).

29. This is Aristotle's statement of the argument. The text, and therefore the details of the argument, are uncertain. But its general nature seems to me to be perfectly clear, and I do not think there is much dispute about it. Its premises are: firstly, the presupposition pointed out by Aristotle, that time is made up of instants, atomic "nows"; and secondly, the assumption that at any given instant a moving body is at a given position, and so at rest. From these the conclusion follows that the moving body must always be at rest, since it is at rest at every instant, and time is composed of instants; for there is, so to speak, no time apart from the instants that make up time and at each of these it is at rest.

This is the general form of the argument: and by it we must be guided in any attempt to reconstruct the text so as to make sense of its details. There are two main difficulties in the text as given by Bekker (i.e. the text here printed, but with the words οὐδὲν δὲ κινεῖται in l. 5 and κατὰ τὸ ἴσον in l. 6 omitted).

(i) ἢ κινεῖται (p. 52, ll. 4–5) does not seem to fit into the argument or make sense.

(ii) p. 52, ll. 5–6. ἔστι...ἐν τῷ νῦν. For reasons I shall give this does not seem to me an adequate premiss from which to draw the conclusion drawn in the next words. And there is a variant reading in some manuscripts: see note to text.

I will deal with these points in order.

(i) Taking the Berlin text reading, ll. 4–5 would translate: "For if, he says, everything is either at rest or in motion when it occupies a space equal to itself." But it seems fairly obvious that this is nonsense. The whole point of the phrase κατὰ τὸ ἴσον must be that it is a definition of rest. So the commentators take it (e.g. Simplicius, p. 52, l. 10: Philoponus, p. 54, l. 6). And if it is a definition of rest then the text which we have is nonsensical— "Everything is either at rest or in motion when it is at rest."[1]

Zeller therefore (*Phil. d. Gr.* 5te Auf. pp. 599–600) proposes to omit the words ἢ κινεῖται, and urges in support of the omission the paraphrase of Themistius (No. 34 below), which certainly seems to suggest at first sight that the words were not in his text. Burnet, *E.G.P.*[3] p. 319, follows Zeller.

On the other hand the words seem quite clearly to have been in Simplicius's and Philoponus's texts (cf. passages Nos. 30 and 33): there is no manuscript authority for omitting them: and I cannot see any reason that could account for their insertion into the text— there seems nothing on which they could be supposed to be a gloss, and the only effect their insertion can have is to turn sense into nonsense.

I therefore prefer to suppose with Diels, not that they are an insertion, but that something has dropped out after them, thus

[1] M. Brochard's attempt (*Études*, pp. 6 ff.) to justify the text of the Berlin edition seems to me simply to ignore this point, and in any case to envisage subtleties unthought of by Zeno. He is followed by Hamelin, *Année Phil.* XVII.

making the text as it stands nonsensical. He suggests (*Vors.* 19. A. 27) οὐδὲν δὲ κινεῖται: and Prof. Cornford in the Loeb suggests alternatively καὶ μὴ κινεῖται.[1] Either of these might easily drop out after ἢ κινεῖται, thus making nonsense of the text; and the insertion of either makes perfectly good sense. Thus taking Diels's suggestion, as I have done, we get the meaning: "For if everything is either at rest or in motion, but nothing is in motion when it occupies a space equal to itself, etc." (p. 53, ll. 5–7).

We may add that Themistius's paraphrase remains a perfectly good paraphrase of the text even when the words οὐδὲν δὲ κινεῖται are inserted. His εἰ γὰρ ἠρεμεῖ ἅπαντα ὅταν ᾖ κατὰ τὸ ἴσον gives perfectly well the sense of οὐδὲν δὲ κινεῖται ὅταν ᾖ κατὰ τὸ ἴσον. The words *may* therefore have been in his text: and if so his omission of ἢ κινεῖται means nothing—it is simply that he does not paraphrase the words εἰ ἠρεμεῖ πᾶν ἢ κινεῖται at all. On the other hand, though the words ἢ κινεῖται seem pretty certainly to have been in Simplicius's and Philoponus's texts, the words οὐδὲν δὲ κινεῖται certainly were not (cf. p. 52, l. 12, p. 54, l. 5), and we should have to suppose them to have been already omitted.

(ii) The argument as so far reconstructed therefore runs: "Everything is either at rest or in motion, but nothing is in motion when it occupies a space equal to itself." What further steps are necessary to reach the requisite conclusion that the flying arrow is at rest? It is absolutely necessary that we should have a premiss which states that at any given instant, ἐν τῷ νῦν, the moving object is κατὰ τὸ ἴσον. The nerve of the argument must be, that what is κατὰ τὸ ἴσον is at rest, and that what is ἐν τῷ νῦν is κατὰ τὸ ἴσον, and therefore at rest. This necessity was clearly recognised by the commentators (Simp. p. 52, ll. 16–17: Philop. p. 54, ll. 6–8, and passage quoted in note 3 to text).

But when we turn to Bekker's text in the Berlin edition we find no such connexion between ἐν τῷ νῦν and κατὰ τὸ ἴσον made. Zeller[2] realised the difficulty and proposed to insert κατὰ τὸ ἴσον after ἐν τῷ νῦν (*loc. cit.*), and so renders the whole phrase "nun ist aber der fliegende Pfeil in jedem Augenblick in dem gleichen

---

[1] I prefer either of these to Lachelier's ἠρεμεῖ δέ, *Rev. Mét. et Mor.* XVIII. 1910.

[2] As also Lachelier, *loc. cit.*

Raume". (Burnet, *loc. cit.*, again follows him.) And this insertion finds some support in the occurrence in some manuscripts of the words τῷ κατὰ τὸ ἴσον after ἐν τῷ νῦν.

This actual alternative reading itself gives us, in effect, the same sense. Prof. Cornford (in a note to the Loeb) proposes that, if we read ἐν τῷ νῦν τῷ κατὰ τὸ ἴσον, we should translate "at every moment the moving thing is occupying the moment (of the time occupied by its whole movement) which corresponds to the space equal to its own dimensions". His note continues, "the time is supposed to be made up of a row of successive indivisible moments corresponding, one to one, with the row of successive positions occupied by the body. τῷ κατὰ τὸ ἴσον was probably added in this MS. to make it clear that ἐν τῷ νῦν means this."

This interpretation gives the necessary connexion between ἐν τῷ νῦν and κατὰ τὸ ἴσον, as does also Diels's suggestion, to insert after ἐν τῷ νῦν in the text πᾶν δὲ κατὰ τὸ ἴσον ἐν τῷ νῦν. And it may be noticed that both Brochard and Hamelin, who try to take the text as it stands, do as a matter of fact in their paraphrases make the connexion. We may in fact say that all interpretations agree in making it, but differ as to how exactly it is to be made. Of the various readings I have, after some hesitation, adopted Zeller's, as giving most simply the sense required and finding some support in the MSS.

As a final analysis of the argument I therefore give the following:

(1) Everything must be either at rest or in motion.[1]

(2) Nothing κατὰ τὸ ἴσον, occupying a space equal to itself, is in motion.

(3) The flying arrow is always ἐν τῷ νῦν.

(4) Whatever is ἐν τῷ νῦν is κατὰ τὸ ἴσον.

(5) Therefore, the flying arrow is κατὰ τὸ ἴσον.

(6) And so (by (2)) not in motion.

(7) Therefore (by (1)) the flying arrow is at rest.

Step (3) clearly depends on what is, as Aristotle points out, the

[1] It will be seen therefore that I disagree with the Oxf. Trans. note *ad loc.*: "Zeno's argument apparently does not prove that the arrow is at rest because it is not in motion." My reasons should be clear from the notes.

presupposition of the whole argument, namely that time is composed of atomic "nows" or instants.

I have already referred several times to the passages from the commentators which follow, and have used them in my attempt to reconstruct both argument and text. And I claim their support in essentials for the version of the argument just given: the differences from it which their versions present are due to compression, omission, or rearrangement, not to any radical divergence.

30. A very compressed statement, with all reference to τὸ νῦν omitted. But quite recognisable. Roughly, steps (1), (2), (5), (6), (7).

31. p. 52, ll. 12–13. πᾶν...ἠρεμεῖ. Cf. above under the note on ἢ κινεῖται, p. 52, ll. 4–5.

p. 52, l. 13. ὅτι...κινεῖται. This premiss does not, it is true, occur in my version: but it does not represent any new departure. It is simply the conclusion to be drawn from (2) and (4) taken together.

p. 52, l. 14. ὅτι...νῦν, i.e. (3), (4) and (5), generalised.

p. 52, ll. 15–16. τὸ φερόμενον...χρόνῳ, i.e. (3), (4) and (5) again, stated with τὸ βέλος as subject.

p. 52, ll. 16–18. τὸ δὲ...κινεῖται. Uses the premiss of p. 52, l. 13 above to prove (6).

p. 52, ll. 18–19. τὸ δὲ...ἠρεμεῖ, i.e. (1).

p. 52, ll. 19–20. τὸ ἄρα...χρόνον, i.e. (7).

I think I can claim with justice therefore that Simplicius's version is merely a rearrangement and not a new departure. The argument is essentially the same.

32. Again omits reference to τὸ νῦν. Contains steps (5), (2) and (7) in that order.

33. p. 54, ll. 5–6. ἅπαν...κινεῖται. Cf. above under the note on ἢ κινεῖται, p. 52, ll. 4–5. The rest simply restates in a different way steps (2)–(7).

p. 54, l. 9. ἀπείροις. Though the atomic instants of which time is supposed to be built up are indivisible, yet there is supposed to be an infinite number of them in any stretch of time (for I take it that τοῦ χρόνου refers to the supposed time of the arrow's movement). This supposition, however, is not an essential part of the argument, and seems rather to be a gratuitous addition of Philoponus's own.

34. Steps (2), (5), (7) in that order.

The commentators thus add nothing, but merely rearrange or compress, as is natural in an explanatory work. My version attempts to follow as closely as possible and to elucidate that of Aristotle himself.

THE STADIUM

The text and interpretation of this argument present greater difficulties than those of any of the other three. I have tried in my notes to the text to indicate what are the possible alternative readings; and in the commentary that follows shall try to justify the version of the text given.

References to Gaye will be to his article in *J. Phil.* XXXI. 1908–10, "On Aristotle, *Physics* Z, IX. 239*b* 33–240*a* 18". My knowledge of Dr Ross's view of the passage is drawn primarily from the note *ad loc.* in the Loeb edition.[1]

It will be seen that of the three commentators, I quote only Simplicius on this argument. Themistius (201. 1) adds nothing to our understanding of the argument; and Philoponus (though I have referred to him on a point of detail, p. 88) completely misunderstands the general sense of the argument (cf. 817. 20, where he supposes there are two stadia, one stationary and one moving).

35. Aristotle's statement of the argument falls into three main sections:

A. 239*b* 33–240*a* 4. General statement of the paradox (p. 54, ll. 15–20).

B. 240*a* 4–8. An illustration given (p. 54, l. 20 οἷον...p. 56, l. 2 τοῖς *B*).

C. 240*a* 9–17. It is shown how, in the illustration, Zeno's paradox is supposed to follow (p. 56, ll. 3–11).

[1] His paper, the loan of which I acknowledge in the bibliographical note to p. 2, contained no detailed account of his views on the text of the passage or its interpretation. But Dr Ross has very kindly answered certain queries of mine by letter.

Section C again falls into three subsections:[1]

 (1) 240a 9–10. συμβαίνει δὴ...κινουμένων (p. 56, ll. 3–4).

 (2) 240a 10–13. συμβαίνει δὲ...ἕκαστον (p. 56, ll. 4–6).

 (3) 240a 13–17. ἅμα δὲ συμβαίνει...γίγνεσθαι (p. 56, ll. 7–11).

The chief difficulty in interpreting the actual argument lies in C (3). For though the meaning of μέσον in A and B and the precise nature of the illustration are questionable, yet it is quite clear what the relative initial positions of the three rows of bodies must be. It is more difficult to see the relation of C (3) to the rest of the argument. With these difficulties I shall deal as I proceed.

Section A

p. 54, l. 16. ὄγκων. ὄγκος = literally the bulk, size, mass of a body: hence a bulk or mass, and so a body. It is certainly a somewhat odd word to use if by it Zeno meant "bodies" simply. The scene is set, so to speak, in a stadium: and it would have been more characteristic of Zeno to have introduced something more in keeping with the scene than the mere colourless ὄγκος (cf. above on p. 50, l. 10). I do not think it likely that the word is due to Aristotle, who has left unchanged the details of the second and third arguments and who would hardly have left στάδιον unchanged while changing some other term to ὄγκοι. Especially as, if my translation of p. 50, l. 10 is correct, he has already commented adversely on the "dramatic" nature of Zeno's illustrations, and would no doubt have welcomed another opportunity for such criticism.

I think therefore (with Gaye, p. 109) that the word ὄγκοι is certainly due to Zeno. And if this is so it certainly calls for comment. It seems most likely that its introduction was due to its having some contemporary reference, a reference to some philosopher or school of philosophers. Tannery (*Science Hellène*, p. 266) followed by Burnet (*E.G.P.*[3] p. 319, note 4) suggests that the reference is to the Pythagorean point-unit-atom. The term ὄγκος would, it is true, fit this quite well; but I think Gaye has shown (p. 110) that there is no real evidence that the Pythagoreans in the time of Zeno made use of it. On the other hand I find Gaye's own suggestion that Empedocles is aimed at entirely unconvincing. All we can say on the

---

 [1] Cf. Gaye, p. 102.

evidence is that it is *possible* that there is a reference to the Pythagoreans. But further consideration of this point must be postponed until a more general consideration of the four arguments as a whole.

p. 54, ll. 16–17. τῶν μὲν ἀπὸ τέλους τοῦ σταδίου τῶν δ' ἀπὸ μέσου. Literally, "some from the end of the stadium, and some from the middle": and from the Greek (ll. 15–17) it appears that we should supply κινουμένων, "some moving, i.e. starting their movement from the end...".

It will be seen therefore that the translation given, which is that of Gaye and the Oxf. Trans., is really more of a paraphrase than a translation. But if we take the conventional view of the meaning of μέσον, namely the middle of the side or length of the stadium,

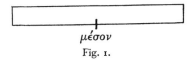

μέσον

Fig. 1.

it is absolutely necessary to give this meaning to the words if we are to get the symmetrical figure which it is quite clear that the argument requires, namely fig. 2.

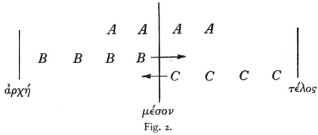

ἀρχή

μέσον

τέλος

Fig. 2.

If the conventional meaning of μέσον is to be kept this must be our initial figure: for on *any* view of the meaning of μέσον the relative positions of the three rows of bodies must be these if the argument is to make sense. (I give no separate justification for this statement. But it should be perfectly clear from the whole treatment of the argument which follows.)[1]

[1] It is perhaps worth noting that Bayle (*Dictionnaire*, s.v. Zénon) has an interpretation in which the initial position of the three rows is asymmetrical. But he is forced to make the two rows start moving at different times, which seems to me unjustifiable; and on his interpretation the

In support of retaining this meaning for μέσον we may first cite the authority of Simplicius. He certainly took it in this sense (cf. his ἀρχομένους μὲν ἀπὸ ἀρχῆς τοῦ σταδίου, τελευτῶντας δὲ κατὰ τὸ μέσον τῶν τεσσάρων A; p. 58, ll. 7–9); and it seems very unlikely that he should have been ignorant of the general lay-out of a stadium. Further, a glance at fig. 2 shows what the real difficulty caused by the words is. The Cs *do* start from the τέλος, and the Bs from the μέσον: but whereas it is the *last* or hindmost of the Cs which is on the finishing line (τέλος), it is the *first* or leading B which is on the middle-line (μέσον). And therefore, if we describe the Cs as starting from the τέλος, the Bs from the μέσον, our description is asymmetrical as between Cs and Bs. Now it is quite clear that Aristotle in lecturing on this argument made use of a diagram, to which he was continually pointing; and this passage is therefore certainly intended to be understood in conjunction with a diagram. If then we suppose him to have used a diagram similar to that given as fig. 2, it does not seem inconceivable that he should have spoken of the Cs starting to move from τὸ τέλος and the Bs from τὸ μέσον, even though the reference is asymmetrical. For his meaning could be made quite clear by pointing; and if he pointed *first* to the τέλος, the μέσον would of course *come next* as he moved his hand or pointer from right to left, and so he might easily describe the position of the Cs by reference to the τέλος, and that of the Bs by reference to the μέσον.

Dr Ross, however, is dissatisfied with this traditional rendering; and takes μέσον in the sense of "the turning point in the double course".[1] Thus:

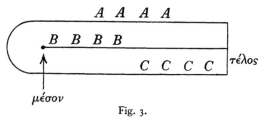

Fig. 3.

argument does not rest on the assumption of indivisibles, but simply on the elementary fallacy Aristotle mentions (*v.* below, p. 54, l. 18), which robs it of its point and destroys its connexion with the other three (see below).

As also does Lachelier, *Rev. Mét. et Mor.* XVIII. pp. 346–7.

So he can translate quite literally "some (moving) from the end of the stadium, some from the midway point". And because it gives the Greek its literal and natural sense his suggestion is very attractive. The difficulty in accepting it is that there is to my knowledge no authority for giving μέσον this sense.[1] I can find no instance of it being so used in any ancient author, and in view of the archaeological evidence it seems to me extremely doubtful whether Aristotle could have so used it. (For this evidence I refer to Gardiner, *Athletics in the Ancient World*, pp. 128 ff.; *Greek Athletic Sports and Festivals*, chs. XII and XIII; and article *J.H.S.* XXIII. 1903, pp. 261 ff.) "Not one of the stadia which have been excavated has revealed any trace of the three pillars or metae forming a line down the middle of the course which were the characteristic features of the Greek hippodrome and the Roman circus, and which still figure in the descriptions and plans which our handbooks and dictionaries give of the Greek stadium" (*Greek Athletic Sports*, *loc. cit.*). And it seems to me that Dr Ross's view loses a good deal of its plausibility if there was no permanent dividing line down the centre of the stadium and so no permanent part of the structure to which τὸ μέσον could refer. Briefly, the stadium may be described as follows. In shape it was rectangular. Starting and finishing line were marked by a line of stone slabs, in which are sockets for posts. These posts seem to have been called καμπτῆρες (note the plural: v. *J.H.S. loc. cit.* pp. 136–7; ref. to *B.C.H.* 1899, pp. 564, 613), and were temporary, having to be renewed each time the games were held (*J.H.S. ibid.*). They seem to have been used both in the stadium-race and in the δίαυλος: in the stadium as objectives, in the δίαυλος as actual turning posts (*J.H.S. loc. cit.* pp. 136–7). In the long races all these posts except the central one were removed, and the runners all turned round it. There was in fact a *single* turning post only in the long races. And I cannot see that τὸ μέσον is a very natural way to refer to it or to the row of καμπτῆρες in the δίαυλος and stadium races. I do not claim that it would have been *impossible* for μέσον to have been used in some such sense as Dr Ross's: but that in view of the archaeological evidence it seems unnatural so to use it and unlikely that it should have been so used. I accordingly prefer to keep

[1] Lachelier admits "cependant je n'ai pu trouver aucun texte à l'appui de cette interprétation".

to the traditional rendering, explaining Aristotle's meaning as I have done above.

p. 54, ll. 17–18. ἴσον...ἥμισυν. The translation given is that of Dr Ross, the Loeb, and Zeller and Burnet.[1] Gaye (*J. Phil.* and Oxf. Trans.) renders: "That half a given time is equal to double that time."

It seems to me that Gaye's claim (p. 101) that this rendering "gives the more natural sense of the Greek" is very doubtful. I think rather that the more natural sense is given by the traditional rendering, though *either* rendering is *possible*. On the other hand his claim (*ibid.*) that Simplicius supports his rendering seems to me definitely unfounded. Simplicius's phrase is "that the same time is both double and half" (which seems to have in its antithetical form a distinctly Zenonian ring): cf. p. 56, l. 17, p. 62, ll. 11–12. This phrase by itself is ambiguous. But he uses it also of the distances traversed (p. 62, ll. 8–9) as well as the times taken; and a glance at the argument of the passage (p. 62, ll. 3–13) makes it perfectly clear that what he means is that one row of bodies has gone *twice as far* as the other. There therefore seems no doubt that Simplicius, when he uses the same phrase of the time taken by the two rows, means that one row has taken *twice as long* as the other. So what the argument proves according to him is that the times the two bodies take, supposed to be equal, in fact stand in the ratio of 2 : 1. In brief, he definitely supports the traditional rendering. So also does Philoponus, 818, 1–9.

But Gaye's strongest argument is that his translation is necessary if any sense is to be made of the last section, C (3), of the argument. And consideration of this must be postponed until we come to this section. For the moment all that can be said is that the translation given has both Simplicius's and Philoponus's authority, and is a perfectly possible and, I think, in fact the most natural rendering.[2]

p. 54, l. 18. ἔστι δ' ὁ παραλογισμὸς κ.τ.λ. The previous arguments, though they may be fallacious, have all turned on points of

---

[1] Lachelier, *Rev. Mét. et Mor.* XVIII. p. 346, translates "qu'une durée est à la fois le double et la moitié d'elle-même", and attaches the same meaning to the phrase.

[2] Cf. Plato, *Charm.* 168 c, οὐ γάρ ἐστί που ἄλλου διπλάσιον ἢ ἡμίσεος: and *Rep.* 479 B. The double is regularly regarded as the double *of the half*.

very genuine logical difficulty and importance. But if Aristotle is right in saying that the present argument turns merely on the very obvious fallacy which he here states, Zeno's reasoning in it is merely puerile. It is however now generally recognised that Aristotle has entirely missed the point of the argument, and that, though the fallacious assumption of which he speaks is made, it is made only as the consequence of another assumption of far greater initial plausibility and far greater logical import. This is, briefly, the assumption that space and time are not continuous and infinitely divisible, but discontinuous and composed of parts or elements that are indivisible ("discontinus et composés d'éléments indivisibles", Noel, *Rev. Mét. et Mor.* i. 1893, p. 107: cf. also Milhaud, *ibid.* pp. 153–4; Tannery, *Science Hellène*, p. 266; Brochard, *Études*, p. 4; Lachelier, *Rev. Mét. et Mor.* XVIII. 1910, pp. 353–4; Gaye, p. 108).

We have already seen that the first two arguments depend on the assumption that space and time are continuous and infinitely divisible; and that the third depends, as Aristotle himself points out, on the assumption that time is discontinuous and composed of indivisible instants. It is not therefore surprising that the assumption of discontinuity of space and time should also underlie the last of the four, thus making the quartet symmetrical. But a further consideration of the point must be postponed until the argument itself has been examined.

SECTION B

p. 54, l. 22. ἀρχόμενοι. "I would draw special attention to the word ἀρχόμενοι, which I take to indicate, not the *point of departure* ('beginning to move'), but the *point from which the eye begins to measure* ('extending'): in fact I very much doubt whether it could have here the former meaning, which would seem to require either a different verb altogether (κινούμενοι or ὁρμώμενοι) or, if ἀρχόμενοι is retained, the addition of an infinitive (κινεῖσθαι) or a genitive (τῆς κινήσεως)", Gaye, p. 103.

p. 54, l. 22. τῶν A. Taking the view of the meaning of μέσον which he does Ross is bound to omit this: and the omission has good manuscript authority.

If we take the view of the meaning of μέσον which I have taken it makes no real difference to the argument whether we retain or omit the words. For the middle of the *A*s must coincide with the middle-point of the stadium (*v.* fig. 4 below), and so we get the same figure on either reading. But we have good manuscript authority for the omission, the words are superfluous and make no difference to the argument, and it is easy to suppose they were added as an explanatory note, which subsequently found its way into the text. Besides, if we omit them, we get a better contrast with ἐσχάτου on p. 56, l. 1. I have accordingly bracketed them, and given a translation expanded analogously to that of p. 54, ll. 16–17 above (on which *v.* note).

The figure we get from this section as the initial position of the three rows of bodies is:

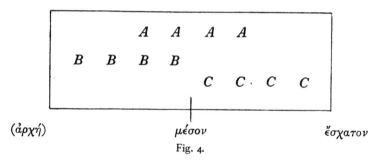

(ἀρχή)   μέσον   ἔσχατον

Fig. 4.

And the following quotation from Gaye will explain how the words of the text describe this figure: "The expression ἀπὸ τοῦ μέσου, like ἀπὸ τέλους and ἀπὸ μέσου above, and ἀπὸ ἐσχάτου below, must be explained by reference to the point of view of an imaginary person standing at the ἀρχή τοῦ σταδίου: that is to say, in their original position the *C*s stretch *from* the end of the course, and the *B*s *from* the middle-point of the course, *in the direction of* anyone occupying that position: thus there will be no reference to the direction of the respective *motions* of the two sets of ὄγκοι" (p. 103: cf. also note on ἀρχόμενοι, p. 54, l. 22 above). In other words Aristotle is not speaking here of the *motion* of the rows of bodies, but simply describing his diagram *statically* reading from right to left. (Cf. what was said above, p. 86, on Aristotle's use of his diagram.)

Section C (1)

p. 56, ll. 3–4. συμβαίνει δὴ...κινουμένων: i.e. this section gives us a figure which results when the *B*s and *C*s move as the argument supposes them to move, in opposite directions and with equal velocities past the *A*s (cf. p. 54, ll. 15–17). I do not think there is any doubt how the sentence is to be interpreted. With ἐπὶ τῷ ἐσχάτῳ we must understand Γ, and with τὸ πρῶτον Γ supply ἐπὶ τῷ ἐσχάτῳ B. The resultant figure then is:

A	A	A	A
B	B	B	B
C	C	C	C

Fig. 5.

Section C (2)

p. 56, l. 5. τὰ B. It will be seen from the note to the text that the manuscripts are divided between the readings τὰ B and τὰ A, and that Simplicius supports the latter reading of the two. If we read τὰ A with him we have to suppose that the following steps have been omitted from the argument.

The first *C* has passed ⟨*all four B*s (v. *fig. 5*): *but the B*s *are equal in size to the A*s: *therefore the first C has passed the equivalent of four A*s, *i.e.*⟩ all the *A*s (cf. Simplicius, p. 59, l. 17 below).

This is rather a roundabout and not too obvious piece of argumentation to leave to the reader to supply; and the reading τὰ B gives more obvious and straightforward sense. On the other hand if we read τὰ B we have to take παρὰ τὰ ἡμίση at p. 56, l. 5 to mean "half that number of bodies, i.e. two *A*s", while if we read τὰ A we can give the words the more natural and straightforward meaning of "half the number of *A*s". But the interpretation "half that number of bodies, i.e. two *A*s" is by no means impossible, especially in an argument so compressed as this—such elliptical methods of expression are only too familiar to students of Aristotle. And I think that the advantage of the simpler interpretation of the phrase which the reading τὰ A gives is far outweighed by the disadvantage of the very awkward interpretation which has then to be given to the previous expression τὸ Γ...διεξεληλυθέναι, which has to suppose several important steps of the argument to have been omitted. If we read τὰ B we need not suppose that any important step has been omitted, but merely that the second step is stated rather elliptically.

I therefore conclude on these grounds in favour of reading τὰ B.

p. 56, l. 5. τὸ δὲ B. I have assumed this reading throughout the previous note. Both the interpretations there given assume this reading: and I cannot see what possible sense can be made of the alternative τὰ δὲ B. τὸ δὲ B has manuscript authority and was read by both Simplicius and Alexander.

p. 56, ll. 5–6. ὥστε ἥμισυν...παρ᾽ ἕκαστον. It is important to understand the precise conclusion expressed in these words, and to see precisely how much and how little is now supposed to have been proved.

The first part of this subsection, C (2), dealt with in the two preceding notes, has drawn from the figure given in C (1) the following conclusions:

(1) The first C has passed all the Bs.

(2) The first B has passed only half that number of bodies, i.e. two As.

The further conclusion drawn in the phrase we are now considering is that the first B has therefore taken only *half* the time to complete its motion that the first C has taken. For the first C and the first B take an equal time to pass each body, and therefore since the first B has only passed half the number of bodies that the first C has passed, the first B has taken only half the time to complete its motion that the first C has taken, i.e. B's time = ½ C's time.

To complete the argument, and show that half a given time is equal to the whole, a further step is needed. It must be proved that B's time also = C's time. Then, since B's time = ½ C's time, and also = the whole of C's time, the requisite conclusion has been reached.

This further step is quite easily taken. But can it with justice be said that it *has been* taken? Gaye's interpretation supposes that it has already been implied in C (1), where it was stated that the first B and the first C reach simultaneously a position opposite the last C and the last B respectively. It is of course *implied*. But then the whole of the succeeding argument is *implied* also. The question to ask is rather, has the step *explicitly* been taken? And the answer is that it has not. Gaye, following Simplicius, can of course *supply* it from fig. 5 in C (1). But a careful study of Aristotle's words shows that all that has *explicitly* been proved is that B's time = $\frac{1}{2}$ C's time.

We therefore naturally expect the remaining step, i.e. that B's time also = the whole of C's time, to be taken in the remaining subsection of the argument. And if it can be shown that this step is in fact there taken, then Gaye's view of the argument must be rejected. In that case the words ἴσον εἶναι χρόνον τῷ διπλασίῳ τὸν ἥμισυν must definitely mean "half a given time is equal to the whole" (cf. note above, p. 88); while the last subsection, C (3), becomes part of the proof of this conclusion, and not the proof of some conclusion beyond it.

Section C (3)

If we keep to the traditional version of the text here—i.e. read τὰ B at p. 56, l. 7 and retain p. 56, ll. 9–10 ἴσον...φησι, as all previous texts have done—it is certainly impossible to get the meaning which I have just argued is required. But from the traditional text it is difficult, if not impossible, to get any meaning whatsoever.

If we read τὰ B at p. 56, l. 7 then we must suppose with Gaye that a third figure is being enunciated in which the Bs and Cs no longer overlap, but have moved clear of each other, and so that ἐπὶ τοῖς ἐναντίοις ἐσχάτοις means "at the opposite ends of the course to those from which they started". His translation of the first phrase (ἅμα δὲ...ἐσχάτοις, ll. 7–9) is (p. 99): "Thirdly, at the same moment all the Bs have passed all the Cs: for the first C and the first B will simultaneously reach the opposite ends of the course." This is a perfectly possible translation of the text. And Simplicius, 1019. 16, 17, seems to support this meaning of ἐσχάτοις (though it should be noted that Aristotle himself has used ἔσχατον not only in the sense of the end of the stadium, p. 56, l. 1, but also in the sense of the end B and the end C, p. 56, l. 4). The figure obtained is then clearly this:

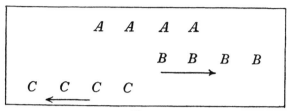

Fig. 6.

But the real difficulties in the interpretation remain. For, in the first place, what is the subject of γιγνόμενον in the following phrase? "It can hardly agree either with τὸ πρῶτον Γ or τὸ πρῶτον B to the exclusion of the other" (Loeb note *ad loc.*); especially in view of the occurrence of the plural ἀμφότερα in the next line. Gaye is compelled to make it agree with τὸ πρῶτον Γ; and this is a very strong objection to his interpretation of the argument.

But even if this difficulty is waived, and a somewhat unnatural grammatical construction allowed, there still remains the task of making sense of the argument. Let us take Gaye's translation of the second (ἴσον...φησι) and third (διὰ...γίγνεσθαι) phrases of the subsection and examine it: "Since (so says Zeno) the time occupied by the first C in passing each of the Bs is equal to that occupied by it in passing each of the As, because an equal time is occupied by both the first B and the first C in passing all the As" (p. 99). Unfortunately he makes no attempt to justify or explain in detail this rendering. But from his statement on p. 105 it appears that he supposes the argument of the second phrase (ἴσον...φησι) to be, that since the first C has passed four Bs, and since it takes an equal time to pass each A and each B, therefore it must have passed four As, i.e. a space = four As, and so be in the position of fig. 6.

But then what are we to make of the third phrase? Syntactically it *should* as far as I can see give the reason for the statements made in the ἴσον...φησι phrase. But Gaye has to refer it back beyond this and see in it a reason for the statement in the first phrase that the first B and the first C reach the opposite ends of the course simultaneously.

It therefore appears that Gaye's interpretation treats both clauses very unnaturally: and I accordingly reject it. With it must be rejected his rendering of ἴσον εἶναι χρόνον τῷ διπλασίῳ τὸν ἥμισυν given above (p. 93). (How the conclusion expressed in his rendering would follow from fig. 6 is obvious from the interpretation of ἴσον...φησι which he gives and which has just been discussed.)

The Loeb translation reads τὸ πρῶτον B at p. 56, l. 7, understands this to be the subject of γιγνόμενον, and consequently is bound to alter τῶν B in l. 9 to τῶν Γ. And for παρὰ τὰ A in l. 10 it reads κατὰ τὰ A. But (1) there is no manuscript authority for the change to τῶν Γ, (2) all the manuscripts and apparently Simplicius (cf. 1019. 20–1) read παρὰ τὰ A, and Alexander (Simp. 1019. 32) reads κατὰ τὸ A: so the authority for κατὰ τὰ A is bad.

The actual translation of the passage in the Loeb is very free and it is not altogether easy to see what relation it bears to the Greek. It omits the words ἅμα γὰρ ἔσται...ἐσχάτοις as a parenthesis and runs as follows: "But during this same half-time the first B has also passed all the Cs (though the first B takes as long, says Zeno, to pass a C as an A), because measured by their progress through the As the Bs and Cs have had the same time in which to pass each other." And this is explained in a note to mean "the first C crosses all the Bs while the first B crosses half the As. Therefore while the first C crosses half the As it will have time to cross all the Bs (as it actually does, by the conditions of the problem). But it takes as long to pass an A as a B or a C. Therefore half the time is as long as the whole time." The note in fact supposes that the purpose of the last subsection is to show that B's time, previously shown $= \frac{1}{2} C$'s time, is also $=$ the whole of C's time. And so far the interpretation seems to me right.

But, as I have already noted, there are objections to the text, and in the translation ἴσον...φησι is rendered awkwardly as a parenthesis in which it is difficult to see much point; while the paraphrase of the last phrase is too free and too obscurely worded to be satisfactory. The interpretation cannot therefore be pronounced entirely adequate.

From the consideration of these two interpretations[1] one point

---

[1] I have considered these two interpretations because a discussion of them seemed to be a convenient way of bringing out the difficulties of the passage. Zeller gives no very detailed exposition. Lachelier's interpretation (loc. cit.) is open to several of the objections I have made against Gaye and the Loeb, and so I forbear to give a separate refutation.

emerges, that it is difficult to fit both the phrases ἴσον...φησι and
διά...γίγνεσθαι into the argument to make sense. The ἴσον...φησι
phrase presents the greater difficulty (as my consideration of Gaye's
and the Loeb versions should have shown): and this throws suspicion
on this phrase rather than the other. Dr Ross accordingly proposes
to omit this phrase as a gloss on the words ἴσον γὰρ ἑκάτερόν
ἐστι παρ᾽ ἕκαστον (p. 56, l. 6). And it is easy to see that it might
be such a gloss—meaning roughly, "i.e. it takes as long to pass a B
as an A", and intended to make clear the meaning of ἴσον γὰρ κ.τ.λ.
by an example. The omission, as we shall see, makes very good sense
of the last subsection; and there is besides a very strong piece of
confirmatory evidence for it. Alexander (apud Simp. 1019. 27 ff.)
gives an alternative reading in which the whole phrase ἴσον...φησι
occurred not in its present position, but after διεξεληλυθέναι at
p. 56, l. 5; and this without doubt makes it look as if the words were
a gloss that had slipped into the text now in one place now in the
other. I have accordingly adopted Dr Ross's suggestion, and
bracketed the clause ἴσον...φησι.

At p. 56, l. 7, for reasons given in the critical notes to the text,
I read τὸ πρῶτον B, instead of τὸ B simply with Dr Ross. As an
additional justification of this reading I may add here that in any
case the meaning required is τὸ πρῶτον B, and that, even if we read
τὸ B, we must, to make sense of the argument, take it to mean
τὸ πρῶτον B. (So Dr Ross in fact translates it as "the first B".)

The last subsection, when the text is thus reconstructed, will now
give us the last step which we saw, in the note on subsection C (2),
is required. The argument may be expanded as follows: "At the
same moment the first B has passed all the Cs, i.e. it has passed four
bodies. But the first C has already (p. 56, ll. 4–5) been stated to have
passed four bodies; and therefore, as B and C each take an equal time
to pass each body, and so an equal time to pass an equal number of
bodies (this is part of the hypothesis of the argument), B's time =
C's time. But it has already been shown (p. 56, l. 6) that B has taken
only half C's time. Therefore half a given time is equal to the whole
of it."

The rest of the subsection, from ἅμα γὰρ to γίγνεσθαι, gives the
reason for the opening statement. "The first B 'has passed all the
Cs' because Bs and Cs move with equal velocities past the As, and so

the first *B* and the first *C* reach the opposite end *A*s (ἐπὶ τοῖς ἐναντίοις ἐσχάτοις: ἔσχατον has already been used in this sense at p. 56, l. 3) at the same time (i.e. the position in fig. 5)."

This completes my detailed exposition of the argument as we find it in Aristotle. Before proceeding to more general considerations, I will first deal with Simplicius's account, given in No. 36. I have already referred to this several times and shall try in wha follows to avoid repetition.

36. The passage printed here is Simplicius's commentary and elucidation of Aristotle's statement of the argument, excluding subsection C (3). His commentary on this last subsection (1019. 10–26) is rather obscure, and misses the point of it entirely (largely because his text was faulty). I have accordingly omitted it.

p. 56, ll. 18–19. διπλάσιόν τε καὶ ἥμισυ. Cf. above on p. 54, ll. 17–18.

p. 56, l. 23–p. 58, l. 21 (1016. 17–1017. 15). *The initial position.* The following diagram summarises Simplicius's view of the initial position:

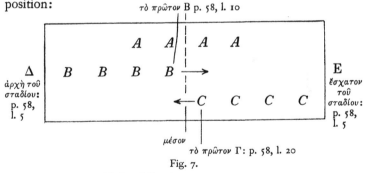

Fig. 7.

To this we may add the following notes:

(1) The number of bodies must be even: p. 58, ll. 1–2.

(2) The *A*s are placed ὡς τὸ μέσον διάστημα ἐπέχειν τοῦ σταδίου ἑστῶτα (p. 58, ll. 3–4): i.e. they are stationary and so placed as to be midway between the beginning and end of the stadium, the first and last *A*s being equidistant from the beginning and end of the stadium respectively.

(3) The *B*s extend from the beginning of the stadium Δ to the mid-point of the *A*s (p. 58, ll. 8–9). And this is the reason why the number of bodies must be even (p. 58, l. 12).

(4) The Cs extend from the end of the stadium E to a point κατὰ τοῦ πρώτου B (p. 58, l. 21), i.e. also to the mid-point of the As.

p. 58, ll. 2–3. ὡς δὲ ὁ Εὔδημός φησι, κύβους. I cannot suggest any reason why Eudemus called the bodies cubes, except that cubes are, as a matter of fact, very convenient for purposes of illustration. For the moving ὄγκοι are of course three-dimensional: and if we take them to be cubes we can represent them two-dimensionally in our diagram easily enough by squares, the square being the side of the cube. Cf. Gaye's method of drawing the figures necessary for the argument:

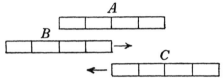

(He actually draws the figure with *eight* squares in each row—but the number is irrelevant.)

This figure with cubes fits very well the "cinematographic" motion I shall describe[1]. Each cube is supposed to move into the *next* cubical place of the same dimensions without passing through any intermediate positions.

p. 58, l. 22–end of passage. (1) *Second position and* (2) *consequences drawn* (i.e. my §§ B and C (1) and (2)).

(1) *The second position*, described at p. 58, l. 22–p. 60, l. 7, is the following:

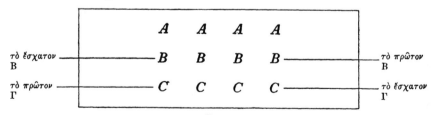

Fig. 8.

p. 58, l. 25. οὐ γὰρ δὴ κ.τ.λ. Simplicius's comment here seems perfectly justified (cf. Lachelier, *loc. cit.* p. 348).

---

[1] pp. 100 ff.

(2) *The consequences drawn* are as follows:

    (i) The first B has passed two As, p. 60, ll. 9–13.

    (ii) The first C has passed four Bs, p. 60, ll. 13–17.

But, since Simplicius read τὰ A at p. 56, l. 5, he goes on to ask what is meant by saying that the first C has passed all the As (p. 60, ll. 17–20), which he takes to mean four As (cf. p. 60, l. 27). His answer to this question may be schematised in the following steps (with what follows cf. note on p. 56, l. 5 above):

    (iii) By hypothesis the Bs and As are of equal magnitude.

    (iv) Therefore since the first C has passed all the Bs, i.e. four Bs, it must have passed all the As, i.e. four As. ((iii) and (iv) = p. 60, ll. 20–2.)

    (v) Therefore (a) of two bodies moving with an equal velocity for an equal time, one has gone twice as far as the other (p. 60, ll. 25–30).

    (b) The time taken by B, assumed the same as C's, is proved to be only half C's, since B passes only two As, C four.

And so, Simplicius concludes, the same distance is both half and double, and the same time is both half and double (p. 62, ll. 8–13: p. 62, ll. 14–end reinforces this conclusion); by which he means that "half the time is equal to the whole time" (cf. above, note to p. 54, ll. 17–18).

Simplicius thus supposes the argument to prove the same conclusion as I have supposed it to prove, but takes the proof to be complete at the end of subsection C (2). This assumption he was presumably led to make by the readings he had of the text of subsection C (3). On his, and indeed on any view of the argument which supposes it to be complete at this point, the last subsection C (3) is merely otiose. And indeed he seems to feel the difficulty in his explanation of it (1019. 10–26), which is not at all clear and of which I am unable to make any good sense. Certainly it adds nothing to our understanding of the argument. I have accordingly omitted it entirely.

I have now given my explanation of the argument. It remains to make a few concluding remarks upon its general nature and the presuppositions it involves.

To assume with Aristotle[1] that Zeno simply committed the
elementary fallacy of supposing "that a body takes an equal time
to pass with equal velocity a body that is in motion and a body of
equal size at rest" is to make the whole argument merely puerile.
If we are to avoid the assumption that Zeno committed this elementary fallacy, the moving bodies in the illustration cannot therefore
be supposed to be behaving like bodies in motion in the ordinary
sense. (This is perhaps suggested by the occurrence of the word
ὄγκοι, see note above, *ad* p. 54, l. 16.)

What characteristics must their motion be assumed to have if the
argument is to be valid? Roughly speaking, the motion must be
supposed to be cinematographic and not continuous. On the
ordinary view of the matter, as the two rows of bodies in the
illustration move past each other some such position as the following
will occur:

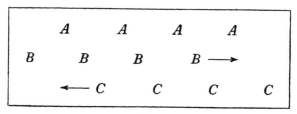

Fig. 9.

i.e. a position in which the various individual bodies *A, B, C* in the
three rows are not in line. For since the ordinary view assumes the
motion of the *B*s and of the *C*s to be continuous, positions such as
this must occur as the *B*s and *C*s move past the *A*s. But for Zeno's
argument it is necessary to assume that no such position is possible,

---

[1] It is worth noting that Eudemus (*apud* Simp. 1019. 33–1020. 6)
supposes Zeno to have committed this elementary fallacy, just as Aristotle
does. His words are (*loc. cit.*): ὁ μὲν οὖν λόγος τοιοῦτός ἐστιν εὐη-
θέστατος ὤν, ὥς φησιν ὁ Εὔδημος, διὰ τὸ προφανῆ τὸν παραλογισμὸν
ἔχειν, εἴπερ ἀξιοῖ τὰ ἴσα καὶ ἰσοταχῆ, ἐὰν τὸ μὲν παρὰ κινούμενον
κινῆται τὸ δὲ παρὰ ἠρεμοῦν, τὸ ἴσον διάστημα ἐν τῷ ἴσῳ χρόνῳ κινεῖσθαι, ὅπερ ἐστὶν ἐναργῶς ἄτοπον· τὰ γὰρ ἀντικινούμενα ἀλλήλοις ἰσοταχῆ
διπλασίαν ἀφίσταται διάστασιν ἐν τῷ αὐτῷ χρόνῳ, ἐν ᾧ τὸ παρὰ ἠρεμοῦν κινούμενον τὸ ἥμισυ διίσταται, κἂν ἰσοταχὲς ἐκείνοις ᾖ.

but that the only possible positions are those in which the various *A*s, *B*s and *C*s are in line: e.g.

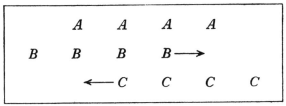

Fig. 10.

Then, if we assume further that the only possible measure of the distance a body has travelled (and so of the time it has been travelling relative to any other body assumed to be travelling at the same speed) is the number of bodies it has passed, Zeno's conclusion will follow.

It is immediately clear that these assumptions involve a view of time and motion similar to that of the last argument (cf. note on No. 28 above). If motion is assumed to have the cinematographic character just described, time must be assumed to be not continuous and infinitely divisible, but discontinuous and made up of instants; for what we mean when we say that motion is cinematographic or discontinuous is that it consists in the occupation of a series of different *positions* at different *instants*. We are thus led to make the assumption that space is composed of minimal atomic parts (extensions, or, as it were, positions), and time of minimal atomic instants: on this the argument rests.[1]

It is easy to see how on this assumption we get the cinematographic type of motion which we have seen is necessary for Zeno's argument.

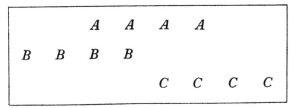

Fig. 11.

[1] As we have seen above (cf. note to p. 54, l. 18) this is now generally agreed. Aristotle elsewhere (*Phys.* Z. 1. 231 *b* 18 ff.) mentions the view that motion takes place in a series of κινήματα, i.e. is cinematographic in the way I have described. A similar view was held by Epicurus: cf. Bailey, *Greek Atomists*, pp. 315–16.

The "bodies" *AA...*, *BB...*, *CC...* must each be supposed to occupy a minimal part of space. Then if their initial position is that in fig. 11, they are supposed *at the next instant* to be in the next possible position, i.e. the *B*s have all moved into the *next minimal space* to the right, the *C*s to the left. And since the only possible measure of distance traversed is number of minimal *spaces* passed, in other words (since the "*bodies*" are supposed to occupy each a minimal *space*) number of "*bodies*" passed, we see that Zeno's conclusion follows.

Actually I think the argument as Zeno framed it was somewhat simpler, and that we can effect the necessary simplification by use of the word "extension". This word (like μέγεθος in Greek) is ambiguous as between what is extended and the space in which it is extended. And so if we understand ὄγκοι to mean "minimal *extensions*" we can see how ὄγκος might have been used ambiguously to mean both the minimal parts of space and bodies which occupy such minimal parts. This ambiguity would suit the present argument extremely well. Zeno would only have to say "suppose three rows of ὄγκοι" and all the necessary presuppositions about minima of space and bodies occupying them would be implied. We have no need to suppose that Zeno could have explicitly formulated these implications. It seems more likely that the idea of space as opposed to what occupies space had not yet been clearly grasped. For we may recall that we have already seen Zeno, in the arguments on plurality, attacking the (Pythagorean) idea of an indivisible element of extension or magnitude, of which the purely spatial and the purely material aspects were not kept distinct; and if the assumption of such an element here makes good sense of the argument we have in the arguments on plurality good authority for making it.

THE FOUR ARGUMENTS ON MOTION. SUMMARY

The first two arguments, we have seen, assume that space, and probably also time, are continuous and infinitely divisible. The third assumes that time is discontinuous and composed of indivisibles, and has as a natural implication that space also is discontinuous. The fourth assumes that time consists of instants, as does the third, and that space consists of minimal extensions. The four in fact form a quartet of which the first two proceed on the assumption of infinite divisibility, the second two on that of indivisibles (cf. Noel, *Rev. Mét. et Mor.* I. 1893, pp. 107–8); and the following passage from Brochard (*Études*, pp. 4–5) expresses clearly their mutual relationships: "Les quatre arguments forment un système d'une curieuse symétrie. Le premier et le quatrième considèrent le continu et le mouvement entre des limites données; le second et le troisième les envisagent dans les longueurs indéterminées et quelconques. Dans le premier et dans le troisième, un seul mobile est chargé de réaliser le mouvement, et il se trouve que le commencement même du mouvement est impossible. Le second et le quatrième, par la comparaison de deux mobiles en mouvement, rendent en quelque sorte plus sensible l'absurdité de l'hypothèse, prouvent que le mouvement, même commencé, ne saurait continuer, et démontrent l'impossibilité du mouvement relatif aussi bien que du mouvement absolu.—Les deux premiers établissent l'impossibilité du mouvement par la nature de l'espace, supposé continu, sans pourtant que le temps cesse d'être considéré comme composé de la même manière que l'espace; dans les deux derniers, c'est la nature du temps qui sert à prouver l'impossibilité du mouvement, sans pourtant que l'espace cesse d'être considéré comme formé, lui aussi, de points indivisibles.—Enfin le second n'est qu'une autre forme du premier, et le quatrième repose sur le même principe que le troisième.—Le premier couple d'arguments est destiné a combattre l'idée qui naturellement se présente la première à l'esprit, celle de la divisibilité indéfinie du continu; le second s'oppose à la conception qui ne s'offre guère à la pensée que quand elle à reconnu les difficultés de la première. L'ordre logique de ces arguments est donc tout à fait conforme à l'ordre historique dans lequel Aristote nous les a transmis et qui était certainement l'ordre adopté par Zénon." This sums up very clearly the connexion and general purpose of the arguments. They form a dilemma in which the possibility of motion is denied both on the assumption of infinite divisibility and on the assumption of indivisibles.

Can we say that they were directed against any school in particular? Zeno's method was to take some presupposition of his adversaries and show that impossible conclusions resulted therefrom. If therefore we take these four arguments to constitute between them a dilemma, then *prima facie* the assumption Zeno is refuting is the ordinary assumption that there is such a thing as movement. This of course as it stands cannot be the tenet of one school rather than another; and it has further been argued that it can hardly be a single school at which Zeno is aiming since the two assumptions underlying the alternatives presented by the dilemma are precisely contrary to each other.

But consider the arguments on plurality. Here we have Zeno arguing that a plurality is impossible both on the assumption of infinite divisibility and on the assumption of indivisibles (cf. No. 11 for example). And we have seen that the reason for this was that he was attacking the Pythagorean point-unit-atom, playing off against each other the assumptions of infinite divisibility and of the existence of indivisibles which it involved (*v.* pp. 32 ff.). Hence the occurrence of these two contrary assumptions in the four arguments on motion seems to me to show not that they were directed against no one school of philosophers, but rather that they were definitely connected with Zeno's attack on the Pythagoreans. And if my interpretation of ὄγκος in the last argument is accepted we have a further and more specific link with Pythagoreanism; for the Pythagoreans did not distinguish clearly between geometrical and physical (cf. above *ibid.*), and it is just this ambiguity which on my interpretation is to be attached to ὄγκος.

I would therefore suggest the following connexion between the four arguments on motion and Zeno's attack on the point-atom: By giving the element of extension the characteristics of point, unit, and atom the Pythagoreans involved themselves in a contradiction, supposing extension to be both continuous and infinitely divisible and discontinuous and composed of indivisibles. In the arguments on plurality Zeno plays these assumptions off against each other. In the arguments on motion the procedure is analogous. Here Zeno is concerned to show motion to be impossible both if extension is continuous and infinitely divisible and if it is discontinuous and made up of indivisibles. The antithesis of infinite divisibility and indivisibles is precisely the same in both sets of arguments:[1] and in

---

[1] Milhaud (*Rev. Mét. et Mor.* I. 1893, pp. 140 ff.) and Tannery (*Science Hellène*, pp. 264 ff.; *Rev. Phil.* xx. 1885, p. 393) both suppose Zeno to have been attacking the point-atom in the arguments on motion; and so

the ὄγκοι of the fourth argument we have an ambiguity of geo-metrical and physical precisely similar to that of the point-atom of the arguments on plurality.

In other words, I suggest that in the four arguments on motion Zeno is using the contradiction inherent in the Pythagorean idea of extension to prove the impossibility of motion, just as in the arguments on plurality he had used it to disprove the possibility of the existence of plurality.

There are further questions involved in this hypothesis which do not fall within the scope of a bare exposition of Zeno's meaning. Had the Pythagoreans a developed theory of motion? Or is Zeno merely bringing out the consequences implicit in their view of extension? And if they had a theory of motion, in what way did they manage to combine in it the two contradictory ideas of infinite divisibility and indivisibles? The most obvious suggestion is that they supposed motion to take place in a series of instantaneous transitions (my "cinematographic" movement), but supposed there to be an infinite number of these transitions in any given motion (just as they supposed the line to be made up of points, but of an infinite number of them (cf. p. 34)). This suggestion in its turn raises the further question: What is the origin and history of this "discontinuous" theory of motion? If my suggestion is correct it was a Pythagorean formulation, arising out of their point-atom theory. But what is the previous history of the idea of continuity, and what is the background of thought on the subject against which the Pythagorean formulation arose? And, whether the Pythagoreans were the first to formulate such a "discontinuous" theory of time and motion or not, what is its subsequent history? For Aristotle certainly refers to a view which regarded space, time, and motion as discontinuous and composed of atomic elements; and a similar view was held by Epicurus.

To answer these questions fully it would be necessary to make a detailed study of the background and development of Pytha-goreanism, of the relevant sections in Aristotle, and of Epicurus; and such an elaborate reference to context falls outside the scope of

far their view would support mine. But they miss this essential antithesis. And I cannot agree with their view of the general purpose of the arguments (v. pp. 65–6 above).

the present study. But some advance has been made to a solution: (1) The four arguments on motion have been shown to contain the same antithesis of infinite divisibility and indivisibles as the arguments on plurality, and to be therefore presumably directed against the same opponents, that is, the Pythagoreans. (2) Whether the Pythagoreans had actually elaborated a theory of motion or not remains uncertain, but if they had done so (and if my interpretation of Zeno's four arguments is accepted), then it must have contained this inner contradiction between infinite divisibility and indivisibles; and the only way in which it could do this would be to suppose on the one hand that motion is discontinuous and takes place in a series of instantaneous transitions, and yet on the other that there are an infinite number of them in any motion.

IV. THE MILLET SEED

THE MILLET SEED

37. Aristotle, *Phys.* H 5. 250a 19; Diels, A 29

διὰ τοῦτο ὁ Ζήνωνος λόγος οὐκ ἀληθής, ὡς ψοφεῖ τῆς κέγχρου
ὁτιοῦν μέρος· οὐδὲν γὰρ κωλύει μὴ κινεῖν τὸν ἀέρα ἐν μηδενὶ
χρόνῳ τοῦτον ὃν ἐκίνησε πεσὼν ὁ ὅλος μέδιμνος.

38. Simplicius, 1108. 18, *ad loc.*

διὰ τοῦτο λύει καὶ τὸν Ζήνωνος τοῦ Ἐλεάτου λόγον, ὃν ἤρετο
5 Πρωταγόραν τὸν σοφιστήν. "εἰπὲ γάρ μοι," ἔφη, "ὦ Πρωτα-
γόρα, ἆρα ὁ εἷς κέγχρος καταπεσὼν ψόφον ποιεῖ ἢ τὸ μυριοστὸν
τοῦ κέγχρου;" τοῦ δὲ εἰπόντος μὴ ποιεῖν "ὁ δὲ μέδιμνος", ἔφη,
"τῶν κέγχρων καταπεσὼν ποιεῖ ψόφον ἢ οὔ;" τοῦ δὲ ψοφεῖν
εἰπόντος τὸν μέδιμνον "τί οὖν", ἔφη ὁ Ζήνων, "οὐκ ἔστι λόγος
10 τοῦ μεδίμνου τῶν κέγχρων πρὸς τὸν ἕνα καὶ τὸ μυριοστὸν τὸ
τοῦ ἑνός;" τοῦ δὲ φήσαντος εἶναι "τί οὖν", ἔφη ὁ Ζήνων, "οὐ
καὶ τῶν ψόφων ἔσονται λόγοι πρὸς ἀλλήλους οἱ αὐτοί; ὡς γὰρ τὰ
ψοφοῦντα, καὶ οἱ ψόφοι· τούτου οὕτως ἔχοντος, εἰ ὁ μέδιμνος τοῦ
κεγχροῦ ψοφεῖ, ψοφήσει καὶ ὁ εἷς κέγχρος καὶ τὸ μυριοστὸν τοῦ
15 κέγχρου." ὁ μὲν οὖν Ζήνων οὕτως ἠρώτα τὸν λόγον.

Cf. 1116. 2, which adds nothing. Themistius, 208. 7, also adds
nothing.

THE MILLET SEED

37. Aristotle, *Phys.* H 5. 250*a* 19; Diels, A 29

Therefore Zeno's argument is not true, that there is no part of a grain of millet that does not make a sound: for there is no reason why any such part should not in any length of time fail to move the air that the whole bushel moves in falling.

38. Simplicius, 1108. 18, *ad loc.*

By this means he solves the conundrum which Zeno the Eleatic 5 asked Protagoras the sophist. "Tell me, Protagoras," he said, "does a single grain of millet or the ten thousandth part of a grain make any sound when it falls?" And when Protagoras said it did not, "Then", asked Zeno, "does a bushel of millet make any sound when it falls or not?" Protagoras answered that it did, whereupon Zeno 10 replied, "But surely there is some ratio between a bushel of millet and a single grain or even the ten thousandth part of a grain"; and when this was admitted, "But then surely", Zeno said, "the ratios of the corresponding sounds to each other will be the same: for as the bodies which make the sounds are to one another, so will the 15 sounds be to one another. And if this is so, and if the bushel of millet makes a sound, then the single grain of millet and the ten thousandth part of a grain will make a sound." This was the way Zeno used to put his questions.

THE MILLET SEED

Aristotle's statement and Simplicius's elucidation of it make quite clear what this argument was, and it calls for no further comment. In spite of its mathematical characteristics I do not think it possible to refer it to any polemic against a definite school.

A word may be said of the occurrence of Protagoras as respondent in the dialogue. Chronological considerations make it quite possible that Zeno and Protagoras may have met. But it is unlikely either that Zeno wrote dialogues or that he would have introduced himself as interlocutor had he written any (cf. *E.G.P.*[3] p. 312).[1] On the other hand the argument is very typical of Zeno and there is no reason to suppose it was not his.[2] It may well have been cast into dialogue form by some later writer, from whom Simplicius here quotes it.[3]

[1] Though against Burnet, it should be noted that Diogenes (quoted *Vors.* 19. A. 14) says definitely that he did. But this may be merely a confusion with Aristotle's statement that he originated διαλεκτική.

[2] Prof. Taylor (*The Parmenides of Plato*, Appendix A, p. 123) is "fairly certain" that Simplicius is not quoting Zeno himself: but thinks it possible that the argument itself may go back to Zeno.

[3] I do not think that we are justified in speaking with Prof. Taylor ("Parmenides, Zeno and Socrates", *Philosophical Studies*, pp. 37–8) of "the well-known allusion of Aristotle to dialogues in which Zeno and Protagoras figured as discussing problems connected with the notion of the infinitesimal". Aristotle makes no explicit reference either to Protagoras or to a dialogue. It is Simplicius (passage No. 38) who gives us the argument in dialogue form. Diels in a note to the passage (19. A. 29), says of the dialogue form "diese Einkleidung stammt nicht aus Zenon... sondern aus einem alten Dialoge (Φυσικὸς des Alkidamas?)".

CONCLUSION

1. In conclusion I should like first to recall the limitations of this study stated in the introduction. I have attempted simply to give as complete a text of Zeno as possible and to explain in the notes what exactly the arguments contained in the text are. I have made no attempt to deal with the logical and mathematical puzzles they involve. Nor have I attempted to examine in detail Zeno's position in the history of Greek thought. Such an examination is of course a natural sequel to an exposition of his arguments; but it is in itself no part of the task of exposition to which I have confined myself.

On the other hand a full exposition of some points has been impossible without some reference to Zeno's historical position. And accordingly I wish, in conclusion, to make a few final comments on this subject, referring briefly to the conclusions already reached in the notes, and suggesting certain further directions in which Zeno's influence is discoverable. What I have to say will admittedly be fragmentary and incomplete; it will raise questions rather than answer them. I shall be content if I have indicated what the problems are and in what particulars Zeno's influence on his successors seems to have been strongest.

2. *Predecessors and contemporaries.* Here I shall merely refer by way of summary to conclusions already stated in the notes.

I. *Parmenides.* Zeno's relation to Parmenides I defined in the Introduction (pp. 6 ff.). He was an orthodox Eleatic, concerned to defend Parmenides by the indirect method of attacking his opponents. Thus we are explicitly told that the arguments in passages Nos. 1–3, attacking the existence of τὰ πολλά, were expressly intended by Zeno to prove, *per contra*, that what is, is one (cf. these passages and the notes to them). This account of the general purpose of his arguments I see no reason to doubt; certainly there is nothing in any of the passages quoted in the text to suggest its falsity.

II. *The "Number-Atomists".* From my examination of the arguments on plurality one definite conclusion emerged (cf. pp. 32 ff.), namely that to make any sense of these arguments we must suppose them to have been directed against a system in which certain definite confusions were made. This system has been conveniently named "number-atomism" by Prof. Cornford (*C.Q.* vols. xvi and xvii): and its essential characteristic is its confusion between the attributes of geometrical point, physical atom and numerical unit. I have further, in my examination of the four arguments on motion (cf. esp. pp. 102 ff.), shown their connexion with Zeno's polemic against this number-atomism. The system was first described by Mm. Milhaud and Tannery: my examination, as will have appeared from the notes, reinforces and in some respects amplifies and modifies their conclusions.

3. *Successors.*

I. *Mathematics and Philosophy of Mathematics.* The most typical feature of Zeno's arguments is the use made in them of the infinite regress. And so after Zeno the problem of the infinite becomes critical for both Greek mathematics and philosophy. It is true that he was not the first to raise it: none the less after him it takes on a new aspect and a new importance. Further, his attack on the point-atom raised acutely the question of the exact nature of point and unit, a question of fundamental importance for the philosophy of mathematics. And it seems not untrue to say that a very great deal of fifth- and fourth-century speculation on the philosophy of mathematics was dealing with the problems which Zeno had been the first to raise. One may instance Socrates's difficulties about the unit in the *Phaedo* (97 A): Aristotle's elaborate discussion of τὸ ἄπειρον,[1] and his careful distinction between point and unit:[2] and the doctrine of ἄτομοι γραμμαί, which was probably elaborated to meet the difficulties arising out of Zeno's attack on the point-atom.[3] The importance of these problems for mathematics and philosophy it is needless to stress.

I think it also quite possible that Zeno's method may have suggested to geometers the proof by *reductio ad absurdum*. This consists essentially in proving a proposition *p* by showing that from its opposite *q* absurd results follow (cf. *A.Pr.* I. ch. 23); which was precisely the method of Zeno, whose aim it was to prove Parmenides's

---

[1] *Phys. Γ*, chs. 4–8; *Met. K*, ch. 10.
[2] E.g. *Phys. E* 3. 227 a 28.   [3] p. 73.

thesis "what is, is one" by showing that the results that follow from the opposite assumption are absurd.

II. *Melissos.* It was natural that Melissos as a fellow-Eleatic should have been influenced by the polemic of Zeno. But what influence we can trace is rather in the form of his arguments than in their content. The typically mathematical interest of Zeno is lacking; and no light is shed on the meaning of Zeno's arguments by the fragments of Melissos. On the other hand in method he does show traces of Zeno's influence. He does sometimes set out to prove his own contention by showing that his adversaries' contention, the opposite of his own, leads to absurd results (e.g. the famous fragment on atomism (Burnet, *E.G.P.*³ p. 323, note 8; R.P. p. 147) where his "if there were a many, these would have to be of the same kind as I say that the one is" is intended as a *reductio ad absurdum* of the pluralists). From the point of view therefore of Zeno's influence in Greek philosophy Melissos is important simply as another exponent of the Eleatic method of reasoning which Zeno had perfected.

III. Εὑρετὴς διαλεκτικῆς.[1] It was as "founder of dialectic" that Zeno's influence was most widely and generally felt; Aristotle has summed up in a phrase what must have seemed to the educated public at Athens to be the real effect of Zeno's argumentation.

To explain and to justify Aristotle's dictum some consideration of the meaning of the term "dialectic" is necessary; and for this we must turn to the *Topics*, which is professedly (100a 21) a handbook on dialectic. In Plato, from its simpler early meaning of the Socratic enquiry by cross-examination, dialectic acquires a more and more specifically Platonic sense as Plato's conception of philosophic method develops. Aristotle, on the other hand, clearly framed his definition with an eye to actual Greek practice. And therefore it is from Aristotle that we shall get the best idea of Zeno's influence, both because in his dictum he was presumably using "dialectic" in his own sense, and because "dialectic" as he uses it refers to a practice general among the Greeks and not confined to any specific school or circle: it is from Aristotle himself that we can best learn what was the dialectic which Zeno was said by him to have founded.

[1] φησὶ δ' Ἀριστοτέλης εὑρετὴν αὐτὸν γενέσθαι διαλεκτικῆς Diog. Laert., Diels, 19. A. 1.

The procedure of dialectic, in the Aristotelian sense, is one of discussion in question and answer form. It would not be easy to find in Aristotle any explicit statement of this very general characteristic. But in the *Topics* as a whole it is clear that it is for verbal discussions of this kind that he is formulating rules; and the greater part of Book VIII in particular is devoted to a consideration of the different rôles to be played by *questioner* and *answerer*. Discussion by question and answer is in fact the method of the dialectic described by the *Topics*. And we may note that in Plato also discussion is an essential part of dialectic. The "maieutic" method which Socrates describes in the *Theaetetus* is one which proceeds by question and answer; and to the end of his life Plato seems to have preferred the spoken to the written word as a method of teaching (*Ep.* II), i.e. discussion of the Socratic type as much as the more formal lecture.

It is further quite evident that Aristotle is laying down rules and formulating methods for an already existent practice. The dialectic of which the *Topics* is a handbook is not his own invention; rather the *Topics* would never have been written if the practice which he calls dialectical discussion had not been widespread and general among the Greeks of his day. For just as the *Rhetoric* presupposes the existence of a class of public speakers and of a public interested in oratory, so the *Topics* presupposes that the practice of discussion which is its subject is a recognised part of social custom. It is true that in the famous last chapter of the *Sophistici Elenchi* Aristotle claims originality for the work he has accomplished in the *Topics*; but the originality which he claims is that of a systematiser and codifier, not that of an inventor. It is not that he has had no predecessors in "dialectic" and "eristic"; but rather that those who have preceded him have never laid down any general rules or subjected their procedure to analysis, but have been content to elaborate and teach particular arguments without further enquiry into principles of reasoning.[1]

[1] Cf. 183*b* 36 ff., where they are compared to Gorgias, who used to describe *particular* ἀρεταί, without enquiring further into the general principles of all ἀρετή (*Meno*, 95*b*; *Politics*, I. 1260*a* 27). Cf. Zeller, *Pre-Socratic Philosophy*, II. pp. 461–2: "The Sophistic teachers proceeded very unmethodically. The different artifices which they employed were collected from all sides, just as they presented themselves; and the attempt was never made to combine these various tactics into a theory, and to arrange them according to fixed points of view."

If Aristotle in the fourth century speaks of these discussions as an established custom of long standing, the dialogues of Plato and Xenophon and the whole career of Socrates are evidence for their existence in the fifth. Socrates could never have lived and taught as he did if he had not had an audience ready to his hand and if discussions like those in which Plato and Xenophon represent him taking part had not been a habit of the Athenian people. The setting of the Platonic dialogue is clearly realistic, even though the actual incidents may be fictitious. And it is this touch with reality and with actual life which, together with Plato's peculiar dramatic genius, gives them their extraordinary vividness. Modern imitations, considered simply as dialogues, are by comparison flat and lifeless simply because such discussions are not a part of our social life at all; and we cannot represent what we have not experienced.

The chief exponents of this art of disputation (apart from Socrates) were of course the Sophists. "We get a vivid picture of the Sophistic art of disputation, as it was constituted in later times, in Plato's dialogue of Euthydemus, and in Aristotle's Treatise on Fallacies; and though we must not forget that the one is a satire written with all poetic freedom, and the other a universal theory which there is no reason to restrict to the Sophists in the narrow sense...yet the harmony of these descriptions one with the other, and with other accounts, shows that we are justified in applying them in all their essential features to the Sophistic teaching."[1] It was under Sophistic guidance that the habit of discussion and disputation was developed and given its characteristic form. Before Socrates and the Sophists the Greeks no doubt discussed; but the discussion as we know it in Plato and from Aristotle, as a regular part of social life, reached its fully developed and characteristic form only in the fifth century under the Sophists.

In their disputations there was no doubt much genuine and serious criticism; but there is also no doubt that they were prepared to court popular applause by the use of any meretricious or ingenious fallacy that would attract attention or bring them success in argument. It is this difference between serious and merely contentious

[1] Zeller, *Pre-Socratic Philosophy*, II. p. 462.

argument that Aristotle marks by his distinction of dialectic and eristic. Dialectic differs from demonstration both in method and subject-matter. In method because, whereas the dialectician must proceed by interrogation, the philosopher and "he who investigates by himself" need not;[1] and whereas the premisses of demonstration must be necessary truths, those of dialectic are merely ἔνδοξα,[2] ἔνδοξα δὲ τὰ δοκοῦντα πᾶσιν ἢ τοῖς πλείστοις ἢ τοῖς σοφοῖς.[3] On the other hand dialectic differs from eristic in spirit rather than in method or substance. For the characteristics in which eristic differs from dialectic are that it is prepared to use as premisses merely φαινόμενα ἔνδοξα, ἔνδοξα, that is, with a superficial appearance of truth only,[4] and to introduce fallacies into the course of its reasoning.[5] In scope and method dialectic and eristic are the same; but "the class-title eristic (or litigious) is founded upon a supposition of dishonest intentions on the part of the disputant".[6] The following outline of dialectic method will accordingly apply to eristic with these qualifications.

Dialectic is a discussion between two persons, one of whom is "answerer" the other "questioner".[7] The thesis[8] for discussion is proposed by the answerer, and is on some subject falling within the realm of ἔνδοξα, the proper sphere of dialectic (roughly, matters of current opinion and interest, as opposed to those requiring more strictly scientific knowledge). It is the answerer's business to defend, the questioner's to attack this thesis.[9] The following paragraph from Grote[10] puts the matter extremely clearly: "Dialectic supposes a questioner or assailant, and a respondent or defendant. The respondent selects and proclaims a problem or thesis, which he undertakes to maintain: the assailant puts to him successive questions, with the view of obtaining concessions which may serve as premisses

---

[1] 155a 7 ff.: cf. 77a 32.

[2] An Post A ch. 2 (for characteristics of premisses of demonstration treated at length): 100a 27.

[3] 100b 21: cf. 104a 11 ff.

[4] 100b 23.   [5] 101a 2.

[6] Grote, *Aristotle*, p. 268.   [7] *Top.* VIII. 1–10.

[8] "Thesis" has also a narrower meaning, cf. *Top.* I. 11, but is frequently used in this sense of the answerer's position on the problem: cf. Oxf. Trans. Index s.v. "thesis" for references, and *v.* esp. 159a 38–9.

[9] 159b 5–6.   [10] *Aristotle*, pp. 270–1.

for a counter-syllogism, of which the conclusion is contradictory or contrary to the thesis itself, or to some other antecedent premiss which the respondent has already conceded. It is the business of the respondent to avoid making any answers which may serve as premises for such a counter-syllogism. If he succeeds in this, so as not to become implicated in any contradiction with himself, he has baffled his assailant, and gained the victory. There are, however, certain rules and conditions, binding on both parties, under which the debate must be carried on. It is the purpose of the Topica to indicate these rules; and, in accordance therewith, to advise both parties as to the effective conduct of their respective cases—as to the best thrusts and best mode of parrying. The assailant is supplied with a classified catalogue of materials for questions, and with indications of the weak points which he is to look out for in any new subject that may turn up for debate. He is further instructed how to shape, marshal, and disguise his questions, in such a way that the respondent may least be able to foresee their ultimate bearing. The respondent, on his side, is told what he ought to look forward to and guard against." Beside this may be set a dictum of Aristotle's own[1] on the functions of questioner and answerer: "The business of the questioner is so to develop the argument as to make the answerer utter the most extravagant paradoxes (τὰ ἀδοξότατα) that necessarily follow because of his position: while that of the answerer is to make it appear that it is not he who is responsible for the absurdity or paradox, but only his position: for one may, perhaps, distinguish between the mistake of taking up a wrong position to start with, and that of not maintaining it properly, when once taken up." This brings out well the essential character of a dialectical debate, the thesis to be defended, the attack by the questioner, the defence by the answerer.

It is not difficult to see the similarity between this "dialectic" method of argument and the method of Zeno. Zeno's method was to take some hypothesis held by his opponents, and to deduce from it conclusions that were self-contradictory. In dialectic also the questioner starts from some thesis laid down by his opponent, the answerer, and attempts by various means to discredit it. And we may note the inclusion among ἔνδοξα of τὰ δοκοῦντα τοῖς σοφοῖς,

---

[1] *Top.* VIII. 4; 159 *a* 18. Quoted from Oxf. Trans. version.

opinions of philosophers, a description which would cover the Pythagorean views attacked by Zeno; in their subject-matter also Zeno's arguments would thus fall within Aristotle's description of dialectic. But the similarity of method is more important. In essence Zeno's method was to confute his opponents by showing that their view contained inherent absurdities and contradictions. In essence the method of dialectic was also to confute an opponent by showing his view to be self-contradictory; "the business of the questioner is so to develop the argument as to make the answerer utter the most extravagant paradoxes that necessarily follow because of his position."[1] It was to Zeno that fifth- and fourth-century dialectic owed its method and spirit.[2]

Some further confirmation may be found in Plato.[3] He speaks frequently of a class of men who construct antinomies (ἀντιλογικοὶ λόγοι), wilful paradox-mongers, whose only aim is victory in argument (cf. *Phaedo*, 90c, 91a). The eristic disputation was evidently well established in the latter part of the fifth century; and at the beginning of the *Sophist* Plato definitely connects this kind of eristic with the pupils of Parmenides and Zeno—οἱ ἀμφὶ Παρμενίδην καὶ Ζήνωνα (216a 3). "Socrates is afraid that a pupil of Zeno will prove 'a very devil in logic-chopping' (θεὸς ὤν τις ἐλεγκτικός) far above the level of the present company, until Theodorus reassures him by the information that the new-comer is more reasonable to deal with than the enthusiasts for controversy (μετριώτερος τῶν περὶ τὰς ἔριδας ἐσπουδακότων, 216b). Plato thus definitely connects the rise of eristic...with the antinomies of Zeno."[4] And one may compare also the remarks in the *Phaedrus* on the "Eleatic Palamedes"

[1] *Top.* VIII. 4, *v.* p. 117 above. Dialectic proceeded by means of verbal question and answer; Zeno, it is true, did not, so far as we know (though it is perhaps worth noting that in the millet-seed puzzle he is represented as so doing). But this does not affect the main issue, that Zeno originated the dialectic method.

[2] The Sophist's dialectic—art of disputation—would have its *practical* use in the courts: for it is even more essential to be able to confute an opponent in a law-suit than in a philosophical argument. But I am here concerned only with its theoretical use in the discussion of philosophical problems.

[3] With this paragraph cf. Taylor, *Varia Socratica*, pp. 91–3.

[4] Taylor, *loc. cit.* p. 92.

(quoted in note to No. 12, p. 32). We have thus further reason to see in Zeno the real founder of the dialectic movement of the fifth century. For "eristic" is merely the bad side of dialectic, and the distinction of dialectic and eristic in Aristotle is not one of subject or method, but simply one between a contentious and a reasonable use of the same method. And the originator of this method was Zeno.

IV. I have so far considered Zeno's position as founder of dialectic very generally; I will now give one or two particular examples of his influence as a "dialectician".

(1) Socrates and Plato. The general method of Socrates in the dialogues of both Plato and Xenophon is "dialectical" in Aristotle's sense. Socrates takes up the position of questioner, elicits from his answerer some "thesis", and finally reduces him to silence by showing him the contradictions involved therein.[1] He is thus in the direct tradition of the dialectic movement, and no doubt his influence in shaping its course was very considerable. Whether he ever actually met Zeno it is unnecessary for my present purpose to decide; but it is at any rate interesting and suggestive to notice that in the *Parmenides* Plato makes Parmenides advise him to practise the typically Zenonian deduction of contrary conclusions from the same hypothesis.[2] But whether direct or indirect, the influence of Zeno is certainly traceable.[3]

[1] Of the Platonic dialogue this description perhaps applies exactly only to the so-called "Socratic" group.

[2] *Parm.* 135 d ff.

[3] Rogers, *The Socratic Problem*, p. 63, notices this influence. But his way of expressing it is unfortunate. He says: "The method of question and answer was not, strictly speaking, new with Socrates; a somewhat similar form of logical argument had been introduced by the Eleatic Zeno as a weapon of debate, and came to be widely adopted alike as a short and easy way of acquiring a philosophic reputation and as a popular form of intellectual diversion." I have no quarrel with the last phrase as a description of eristic, its place in fifth-century discussion, and its origin with Zeno. But Rogers has noted as a "similarity" a characteristic in which the Socratic and Zenonian methods were almost certainly dissimilar. For Zeno did not as far as we know proceed by verbal question and answer. This, however, would not affect the main issue of the influence of Zeno's method on Socrates: cf. p. 118, note 1.

The Platonic dialectic in its final form contained many elements not Socratic, but there was undoubtedly a strong Socratic element in it to the end[1] and in this way, through Socrates, Zeno influenced Plato. So Prof. Taylor writes of the "method of hypothesis" in the *Phaedo*: "We can see, moreover, from what quarter Socrates is likely to have derived the suggestion of the method. Rigorous deduction of the consequences of an hypothesis was the peculiar method of the famous Zeno of Elea, though it was the hypothesis of his opponents which he treated in this way, and his object was to discredit them by showing that they led to impossible consequences."[2] In the influence of the Socratic elenchus on Plato we may trace indirectly the influence of Zeno.

(2) Gorgias. "Gorgias had been driven by Eleatic dialectic to give up all belief in science"; Burnet[3] thus sums up the more strictly philosophical side of Gorgias's teaching. This is to be found in his Περὶ Φύσεως ἢ τοῦ μὴ ὄντος, preserved by Sextus,[4] and in the similar account of his beliefs in Aristotle's *M.X.G.*[5] Gorgias attempted to prove (1) that there is nothing, (2) that even if there is anything, we cannot know it, (3) that even if we could know it, we could not communicate our knowledge to anyone else. And the arguments which he uses in his attempted proofs of these three theses are in form strongly reminiscent of Zeno. We may instance Sext. *adv. Math.* VII. 66,[6] ὅτι μὲν οὖν οὐδέν ἐστιν ἐπιλογίζεται τὸν τρόπον τοῦτον· εἰ γὰρ ἔστι ⟨τι⟩, ἤτοι τὸ ὂν ἔστιν ἢ τὸ μὴ ὄν, ἢ καὶ τὸ ὂν ἔστιν καὶ τὸ μὴ ὄν; in which we notice the adoption of the adversaries' premiss (εἰ γὰρ ἔστι τι) and the statement of conflicting alternatives therein involved. And this passage is typical of the whole. In substance also there are traces of Zeno's influence. There is the argument on space, referred to above (p. 38), at VII. 70: there is at VII. 73 an argument from infinite divisibility, at VII. 74 an argument about ἕν and πολλά, both of which recall similar arguments in Zeno. It seems in fact fairly certain that Gorgias drew

---

[1] Cf. Cornford, "Mathematics and Dialectic in the Republic, VI–VII" (*Mind*, N.S. vol. XLI), for a discussion of Socratic and non-Socratic elements in Plato's dialectic.

[2] Taylor, *Socrates*, p. 161. [3] *Greek Philosophy*, p. 119.

[4] *Adv. Math.* 65 ff.; Diels, 76. B. 3. [5] 979a 11–980b 21.

[6] *Apud* Diels, *loc. cit.*

his method and his arguments very largely from Zeno.[1] And it is important to notice the completely negative result to which Gorgias is led by Zeno's critical methods. For the fifth century was a century of growing scepticism, a century in which existing standards were questioned and existing institutions criticised. And there can be no doubt that in this process Zeno's influence was strongly on the side of scepticism. His own conclusions—that there is no plurality and no motion—are, manifestly, calculated to inspire it; and, more important, it was he who supplied dialectic with its critical method. Philosophically the outcome was, as we see in Gorgias, complete scepticism; and the effect on ethics and standards of conduct was analogous.

(3) Protagoras. There is some plausibility in Burnet's[2] suggestion that Protagoras in his doctrine "man the measure" was maintaining the practical standards of common sense against the theoretical scepticism of Zeno; for the champion of νόμος was likely to be also the champion of common sense. But a more direct influence is to be found in Protagoras's dictum about the δύο λόγοι—καὶ πρῶτος ἔφη δύο λόγους εἶναι περὶ παντὸς πράγματος[3]—which seems certainly to owe its origin to Zeno. It would be a natural inference to draw from his arguments with their two contradictory conclusions; and Plato[4] seems to suggest an Eleatic origin for the eristic habit of constructing antinomies. (It is interesting to note in this context that there was a tradition that Protagoras and Zeno actually met: cf. No. 38, the falling millet seed.)

Protagoras himself, if we can trust Plato on this matter, does not seem to have drawn any very revolutionary conclusions from these two doctrines, but rather to have used them to argue in favour of νόμος, to justify rather than to criticise social institutions—"so far from being a revolutionary, he was the champion of traditional morality, not from old-fashioned prejudice, but from a strong belief in the value of social conventions";[5] but the doctrine that there are

---

[1] Cf. *M.X.G.* 979a 22 τὰ μὲν ὡς Μέλισσος, τὰ δὲ ὡς Ζήνων ἐπιχειρεῖ δεικνύειν. And we have already noticed Melissos as an exponent of Zeno's method.

[2] *G. Ph.* p. 114. [3] Diog. Laert. IX. 51, *apud* Diels, 74. A. 1.

[4] Above, p. 118. [5] Burnet, *G. Ph.* p. 117.

two λόγοι on every question and the method of constructing
antinomies could as easily be used to point the arbitrariness of
human institutions and the apparent lack of any absolute moral
standards. This must have been the effect (if not the purpose) of
such works as the Δισσοὶ Λόγοι.

(4) The Δισσοὶ Λόγοι. Protagoras's dictum about the δύο
λόγοι can thus in all probability be traced to Zeno: Zeno deduced
from his adversaries' hypotheses contrary conclusions, producing
an "antinomy", and Protagoras drew the inference that it is
always possible to construct such an antinomy on any question.
And when Plato refers to the method of ἀντιλογία, the construction
of antinomies, he seems to connect the method with the Eleatics—
again the relation to Zeno's two conclusions is obvious. It is
therefore reasonable to conclude that this particular habit of fifth-
century dialectic, the construction of antinomies, takes its origin
from Zeno.

The Δισσοὶ Λόγοι, a product of late fifth-century Sophistic,
gives us an example of this antinomian type of argument. The
method is to take a pair of contradictory assertions (e.g. the first
pair: good and evil are different, good and evil are identical) and
to give arguments in favour of both. Unfortunately the work is
fragmentary and we cannot be certain what the author's intention
was. But the effect left on the mind is that on any subject no belief
is any truer than its contradictory, in ethics (its main concern) that
there is no real distinction between right and wrong, it is just a
matter of chance opinion. And I think Prof. Taylor is probably
right when he suggests some such sceptical conclusion to have been
intended by the author.[1] The work thus gives chapter and verse for
many of Plato's accusations against the Sophists, and shows what

---

[1] *Varia Socratica*, p. 120. I doubt if the object of the work is specifically
"to reinforce the Eleatic doctrine that τὰ πολλά, the contents of the world
of sensible experience, are unknowable". It was undoubtedly Zeno's
influence that produced this antinomy-construction: but that influence
spread beyond the Eleatic school and I can see no reason to suppose the
author of the Δ.Λ. to have been an Eleatic, interested in reinforcing the
Eleatic doctrine. On the other hand I entirely agree with Prof. Taylor's
more general formulation of the purpose of the work, to show "that no
belief...is any truer than its contradictory".

a powerful weapon Zeno had put into the hands of fifth-century criticism.

4. In these final remarks I have first briefly indicated the conclusions arrived at in the notes on Zeno's relations to Parmenides and to the Pythagoreans. I have spoken even more briefly of his place in the history of Greek mathematical philosophy, and of his influence on Melissos. Finally I have dealt more at length with his position as "founder of dialectic", showing how the Sophistic dialectic and eristic owes its method to him, and tracing one or two more particular influences in Socrates and Plato, in Gorgias, Protagoras, and the fifth-century construction of antinomies. I make no claim to have exhausted the subject; and I am more particularly aware of the inadequacy of my treatment of the question of Zeno's place in the history of Greek mathematical philosophy. But I hope that, though I have not exhausted the subject, I have at any rate indicated what is its nature and extent.

APPENDIX

BIBLIOGRAPHY[1]

In the Bibliographical Note on p. 2 I have given a list of the books and articles most relevant to the historical study of Zeno, most relevant, that is, to a study whose object is to find out what the arguments of Zeno were and what the form in which he expressed them; I append here a more comprehensive bibliography, to include those whose interest lies in the mathematical and logical difficulties raised by the arguments as much as in their historical interpretation.

BAYLE. *Dictionnaire* s.v. Zénon.

BROAD, C. D. *Mind*, N.S. XXII. 1913, pp. 318–19.

BROCHARD, V. *Séances et Trav. de l'Acad. des Sc. Mor. et Pol.* N.S. XXIX. I. pp. 555–68.

—— *Rev. Mét. et Mor.* I. 1893, pp. 209–15.
   These two articles are reprinted in his *Études de Philosophie Ancienne et Moderne*.

BURNET, J. *Early Greek Philosophy*, ed. 3, pp. 310 ff.

CAJORI, F. "History of Zeno's Arguments on motion", *American Math. Monthly*, XXII (1915), pp. 1–6, 39–47, 77–82, 109–15, 143–9, 179–86, 215–20, 253–8, 352–7.

CONTURAT, L. *Rev. Phil.* XXXIII. 1892, pp. 314–15.

DUNAN, C. *Zenonis Eleatici Argumenta* (Nannentibus, 1884).

EVELLIN, F. *Rev. Mét. et Mor.* I. 1893, pp. 382–95.

FRONTERA, G. *Études sur les arguments de Z. d'É.* (Paris, 1891).

—— *Rev. Phil.* XXXIII. 1892, pp. 311–14.

GAYE, R. K. *J. Phil.* XXXI. 1908, pp. 94–116.

GERLING. *De Zenonis paralogismis motum spectantibus* (Marburg, 1825).

[1] I must acknowledge the help I have received in compiling this bibliography from a bibliography sent to me by Dr Ross.

HAMELIN, O. *Année Philos.* XVII. 1907, pp. 39–44.

HEATH, T. L. *Greek Mathematics,* vol. I. pp. 273–83.

JOURDAIN, P. E. B. *Mind,* N.S. XXV. 1916, pp. 42–55.

LACHELIER, J. *Rev. Mét. et Mor.* XVIII. 1910, pp. 345 ff.

LECHELAS, G. *Rev. Mét. et Mor.* I. 1893, pp. 396–400.

MILHUAD, G. *Rev. Mét. et Mor.* I. 1893, pp. 151–6, 400–6.

—— *Les Philosophes-Géomètres de la Grèce* (Paris, 1908), pp. 130 ff.

MOURET, G. *Rev. Phil.* XXXIII. 1892, pp. 67–71.

NOEL, G. *Rev. Mét. et Mor.* I. 1893, pp. 108–25.

PETRONIEVICS, B. "Zenos Beweise gegen die Bewegung", *Archiv f. Gesch. d. Phil.* XX. 1906.

RENOUVIER, C. B. *Esquisse d'une classification systématique des doctrines philosophiques* (Paris, 1885), vol. I. pp. 34–9.

RUSSELL, B. *Principles of Mathematics* (Cambridge, 1903), pp. 347–60.

—— *Our knowledge of the external world,* pp. 129–37, 165–82.

SALINGER, R. *Archiv f. Gesch. d. Phil.* 1906, pp. 99–122.

TANNERY, P. *Pour l'histoire de la Science Hellène* (2me éd. Paris, 1930), pp. 255–70.

—— *Rev. Phil.* XX. 1885, pp. 385–410.

WELLMANN, E. *Zenos Beweise gegen d. Bewegung u. ihre Widerlegungen* (Frankf. a. O. 1870).

WICKSTEED, P. AND CORNFORD, F. M. *Aristotle's Physics,* vol. II (Loeb ed.).

ZELLER, E. *Philos. d. Grieschen,* vol. II. I. ed. 6, pp. 755–65. Eng. Trans: *Pre-Socratic Philosophy,* vol. I, pp. 608 ff.

To this bibliography should be added

ROSS, W. D. *Aristotle's Physics,* esp. pp. 71–85, 655–666, which was published too late for me to be able to use or refer to it.

Made in the USA
Middletown, DE
30 June 2021